QUICK ESCAPES® FROM
Houston

Help Us Keep This Guide Up-to-Date

We would love to hear from you concerning your experiences with this guide and how you feel it could be improved and kept up-to-date. Please send your comments and suggestions to:

editorial@GlobePequot.com

Thanks for your input, and happy travels!

Quick Escapes® From series

QUICK ESCAPES® FROM
Houston

. . . .

The Best Weekend Getaways

FIRST EDITION

Kristin Finan

travel

Guilford, Connecticut

All the information in this guidebook is subject to change.
We recommend that you call ahead to obtain
current information before traveling.

Editor: Amy Lyons
Project editor: Kristen Mellitt
Layout: Melissa Evarts
Text design: Sheryl P. Kober
Maps: Design Maps Inc. © Rowman & Littlefield Publishing Group

Library of Congress Cataloging-in-Publication Data is available on file.
ISBN 978-0-7627-5400-7

Printed in the United States of America

For my parents, who have been encouraging me to see new places ever since I was a toddler; for my husband, Patrick, who has been by my side for the best adventures of my life; and for my daughter, Kona Isabelle, my very favorite travel partner.

ABOUT THE AUTHOR

Kristin Finan is the travel writer for the *Houston Chronicle* newspaper in Houston, which she thinks is the most underrated city in Texas. She enjoys breakfast tacos, Real Ale beer, swimming holes, dance halls, and singing along to the radio in the car with her daughter.

ACKNOWLEDGMENTS

I'd like to thank all of the people who helped with the research for this book, from hotel managers to restaurant owners to convention and visitors bureaus to friends who detailed their favorite places with me at length. I'd particularly like to thank RoShelle Gaskins of the Galveston Island Convention and Visitors Bureau, the Lake Charles/Southwest Louisiana Convention and Visitors Bureau, and Dancie Perugini Ware Public Relations, as well as Monica Haas, Rachel Gale, Benjamin Finan, Cookie Roberts, K. J. Joshi, Amora Rodrigues, and Patrick Cowherd for their advice and assistance. I'd also like to thank my agent, Julie Hill, and editor, Amy Lyons, for the consistent help, guidance, and confidence.

CONTENTS

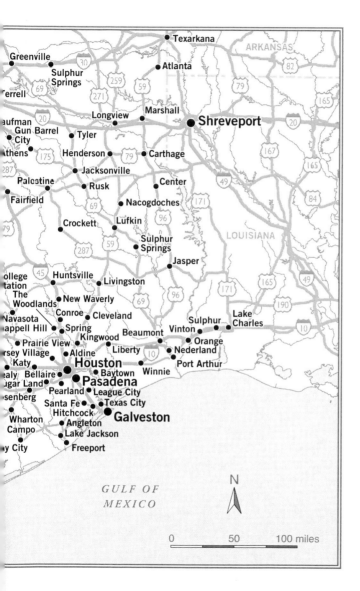

INTRODUCTION

Six years ago, I moved to Houston begrudgingly, knowing little about it other than that it had a reputation for horrendous traffic, smog, and sprawl.

Within just a few months of living here, however, I realized one of this city's major charms: Go an hour or two in any direction, and you'll find yourself transported to a completely different environment.

Going north? Get ready for gorgeous piney woods.

West? Explore the rolling hills of the Texas Hill Country.

East? Have an adventure with airboats and alligators in Cajun territory.

South? Enjoy the lovely beaches.

There's no shortage of ways to escape the city for a weekend. The only trick is knowing what to do once you get there.

That's where this book comes in. I've put together seventeen weekend escapes that offer detailed itineraries, from where to eat breakfast to little-known attractions to the best places to stay. Follow them exactly, or pick and choose the parts that seem the most fun. Either way, you won't go wrong with these suggestions.

The book is broken down into five sections: Westbound Escapes, Northbound Escapes, Southbound Escapes, Eastbound Escapes, and Central Escapes. The trips range from one- to two-night stays and encompass major cities such as Austin and Dallas as well as small towns such as Lockhart and Gruene. Most of the destinations are accessible via the major highways that cross Houston: I-10, I-45, US 290, and US 59.

While these itineraries are certainly complete, don't be afraid to go off the beaten path if you see something interesting. Some of my favorite times researching this book came when I stopped at an inconspicuous barbecue shack or took a chance on a funky-sounding museum. Remember, it's about the journey, not the destination.

You'll find addresses, phone numbers, and websites for places listed throughout the book. In the interest of accuracy and because they are subject to change, the hours of operation and attraction prices are given in general terms. Always remember to call ahead or check the websites of the places you're visiting to see if any of their basic information, hours, or admission rates have changed. A business's website is frequently the quickest, most up-to-date way to find this information.

You can assume all establishments listed accept major credit cards unless otherwise noted. If you have questions, contact the establishments for specifics.

Additionally, most restaurants and lodgings listed here are in the midrange pricewise; I did not include rates and prices, as they frequently change.

In addition to the restaurants, lodging, and activities I've suggested, there are also many more options, so at the end of each chapter, I've included lists of more things to do, special events and festivals, additional restaurants and lodgings, and important informational links. I recommend researching them on your own and calling in advance if you decide to go.

It's also a smart idea to make your lodging reservations well in advance, as they can book up quickly at certain times of the year. I've tried to note most restaurants that require reservations, but if a place seems like it might call for them, it doesn't hurt to phone ahead before you go.

Before you head out for your trip, there are also a few things you should pack, just in case:

- **Sunscreen.** Many of these attractions are outdoors, and we all know how hot that Texas sun can get.

- **Tennis shoes.** Many swimming holes, parks, and trails have uneven terrain.
- **Wet wipes.** Good for cleaning barbecue-sauce-soaked hands.
- **Bug spray.**
- **Maps.** The directions included here are general, so you'll want to be sure to have your own maps as well.
- **A flashlight.**
- **Cash.** Many smaller museums and restaurants still only accept cash, and it's also handy for any tolls you may encounter.
- **A rain jacket or umbrella.** Summers in particular are known for being unpredictable weatherwise.
- A **Texas State Parks Pass,** which will allow you entry into state parks and historic sites without paying entrance fees. The cost is $60 for one year. Buy the passes at most state parks, or call (512) 389-8900.
- **Snacks.** Should you get lost, it doesn't hurt to have some snacks on hand. Grab some bottled water and trail mix as you head out.
- **iPod.** A road trip wouldn't be complete without great tunes.

Feel prepared? Good. Now hit the road. You've got miles and miles of Texas to see.

WESTBOUND
ESCAPES

WESTBOUND ESCAPE *One*
Brenham and Chappell Hill
ICE CREAM, WILDFLOWERS, AND WINERIES—OH, MY—
IN BRENHAM / 1 NIGHT

- Blue Bell Creamery
- Wildflowers
- Charming town square
- Quaint shops
- Laid-back lodging

Nestled within rolling hills that spend much of the year covered in a mosaic of bluebonnets, Indian paintbrushes, and other Texas wildflowers lies the city of Brenham. A quaint, charming little town that exemplifies country living at its finest, Brenham lies a short seventy-five-minute drive down US 290.

The biggest attraction in Brenham is the Blue Bell Creamery, where workers are known to "eat all they can and sell the rest." But more than just the creamery, this city surprises and entertains all ages with its mix of country fare, eclectic antiques shops, and pure beauty. A weekend here in Brenham is sure to leave you relaxed, rejuvenated, and excited about this slower paced way of life outside the big city.

DAY 1/MORNING

BREAKFAST   To get to Brenham, simply take US 290 for about 75 miles and, voila, you're there. On the way, stop for breakfast at **Shipley's Doughnuts** (14135 US 290; 713-690-7610; www.shipleydonuts.ws), a Texas-based chain that has been "making life delicious" with its fresh cake, filled and yeast doughnuts, and strong coffee since 1936. Don't miss the warm apple doughnut, which oozes gooey filling almost like you're eating a cobbler, or the chocolate iced cake doughnut, which practically melts in your mouth when you bite into it.

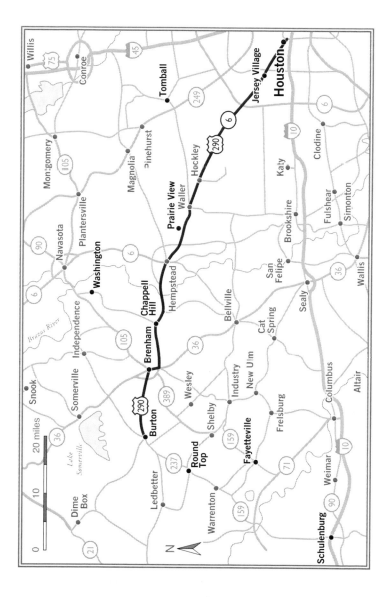

More a fan of kolaches (aka: filled German pastries made in sweet and savory varieties)? Then stop at the **Chappell Hill Exxon and Bakery** (8990 US 290, 979-836-2560), a gas station serving tender kolaches in a variety of flavors.

Once you get close to Brenham, exit on TX 6 at Hempstead and take that to Navasota. From Navasota, take TX 105 west 7 miles and go left on FM 1155 until you reach the **Washington-on-the-Brazos State Historic Site** (FM 1155 in Washington; 936-878-2214; www.tpwd.state.tx.us), a 293-acre park located in the site where the original town of Washington was founded. Admission to the park is free.

Make your first stop inside the park the **Barrington Living History Farm** (21300 Park Road 12 in Washington; 936-878-2214; www.tpwd.state.tx.us), a working farm where you can interact with interpreters dressed in clothes similar to what would have been worn in the nineteenth century. Learn from them how to harvest crops, tend to the animals, or even make soap. All of this takes place at the actual home of the farm's original residents. Open daily from 10 a.m. to 4:30 p.m.

Then, head over to the **Star of the Republic Museum** (17700 Pickens Rd. in Washington; 936-878-2461; www.starmuseum .org), which celebrates the ten years that Texas was its own republic. Run by Blinn College and featuring exhibits, artifacts, photos, and demonstrations that tell the story of that time, the museum is a must-see for anyone interested in the fascinating history of this state. Don't miss the Showers Brown Discovery Center, which offers hands-on educational activities and interactive displays to help children (and their parents) learn about the republic. Open from 10 a.m. to 5 p.m. daily.

Had your fill of history? Go right on FM 1155 and take that until you reach TX 105. Go east until you reach the **Monastery of St. Clare** (9300 Hwy 105 in Brenham; 979-836-9652; www

.monasteryminiaturehorses.com). OK, so I know what you're thinking: "What am I doing at a monastery on my vacation?" Hear me
out. It may sound bizarre, but this monastery is also a miniature
horse farm that is open to the public. "You may be coming to see
the miniature horses," the website says, "but the journey is a spiri-
tual one. Come out. Come often." As you tour the property, wandering in and out of the pens of more than sixty pint-size gray, brown,
and spotted horses no bigger than your average dog, you can't help
but find yourself charmed by this place. The farm is open to visitors
from 1:30 to 4 p.m. Tues through Sat. Admission is $4 for adults,
$2 for children 3–12, and $3 for seniors.

LUNCH When your stomach starts growling, take TX 105 southwest
8 miles until you reach E. Main Street and go right. Then, go left on TX 36 BR/South
Austin Street, left on W. Alamo Street, and end at **Must Be Heaven Sandwich Shop**
(107 W. Alamo St.; 979-830-8536; www.mustbeheaven.com). Know for its big sandwiches and its even bigger slices of pie, this great little restaurant is the perfect
place for a lunch pit stop. Don't miss the turkey club, which is almost 6 inches tall,
or the incredible apple pie topped with a big scoop of Blue Bell vanilla ice cream.
Open 8 a.m. to 5 p.m. Mon through Sat and 11 a.m. to 3 p.m. Sun.

Want something off the main square? Try the Brenham Municipal Airport's
Southern Flyer Diner (3001 Aviation Way; 979-836-5462; www.brenhammunicipal
airport.com), an odd yet surprisingly good little diner where everything is made from
scratch, from the chile with corn bread to the fried catfish to the award-winning
hamburgers.

AFTERNOON

Since there's always room for ice cream, go east on W. Alamo until
you reach S. Blue Bell Road and go right until you see the **Blue Bell
Creamery** (1101 S. Blue Bell Rd.; 800-327-8135; www.bluebell

.com), which has been serving some of the creamiest stuff in the state (and now the country) since 1907. The forty-five-minute tour gives you a nice history lesson on the company, interesting facts about the ice cream (did you know, for example, that despite the variety of flavors offered, the most popular continues to be Home-made Vanilla?), a tour of the plant, and a serving of ice cream at the end. Tours are offered Mon through Fri at 10 a.m., 11 a.m., 1 p.m., 1:30 p.m., 2 p.m., and 2:30 p.m. No tours are offered on weekends. Admission is $5 for adults, $3 for seniors 55 and up, and $3 for children 6–14.

Next, walk off that ice cream with some shopping at the many wonderful stores in Brenham. Start at the **Antique Rose Emporium** (10000 FM 50; 979-836-9051; www.antiqueroseemporium.com), a gorgeous garden and flower shop that hosts special events such as herb seminars, tomato tastings, and cooking classes. Next, visit **Leftovers Antiques** (390 US 290; 979-830-8496; http://leftovers antiques.net), a beautiful showroom with objects collected from around the globe. Upholstery, bedding, and bath items are also available. Open daily from 10 a.m. to 6 p.m. Finally, check out **Westwood Gifts** (2160 US 290; 979-830-0830; www.westwood gifts.com), a fun little gift shop selling Yankee candles, specialty jewelry, framed art, wind chimes, clocks, and more.

Your official shopping may be over, but there's a good chance you'll want to pick up a few items at your next stop, located off US 290 at FM 1155 north. Take 1155 north until it dead-ends, then go right until you reach Dillard Road and see **Chappell Hill Lavender Farm** (2250 Dillard Rd.; www.chappellhilllavender.com). Here, you can cut your own lavender for $5 a bunch, tour the grounds, and purchase lavender-infused products. Open Sat from 9 a.m. to 5 p.m., Sun from 11 a.m. to 5 p.m., and weekdays by appointment.

After that, travel south on FM 1155 to US 290 and go right. Take that to TX 36 and go left, then go right on Salem Road until you reach **Pleasant Hill Winery** (1441 Salem Rd.; 979-830-8463; www.pleasanthillwinery.com), a local favorite that offers a full list of reds and whites. Open 11 a.m. to 6 p.m. Sat and noon to 5 p.m. Sun. Tours are $3 per person for a tour and tasting of four wines. Or try out **Windy Winery** (4232 Clover Rd.; 979-836-3252; www.windywinery.com), a small winery that packs a powerful punch. Open Sat from 11 a.m. to 5 p.m. and Fri and Sun from noon to 5 p.m.

DINNER   Soak up that wine with a delicious dinner. Take FM 1155 until you see Champion Drive and take that to the **Inn at Dos Brisas** (9400 Champion Dr.; 979-277-7750; www.dosbrisas.com), an immaculate inn featuring a five-star restaurant serving organic, fresh dishes that combine "a French chef's passion for quality, an American flair for presentation, and an appreciation of Asian minimalist technique." It also has one of the largest wine selections in the state. The inn is open for dinner Thurs through Sun from 5 to 10 p.m.

If that sounds too intimidating, you can always head to **Ernie's** (103 S. Baylor St.; 979-836-7545; www.erniesrestaurant.com), a classic American bistro with fare such as grilled Atlantic salmon, grilled bobwhite quail, and grilled seven-ounce sirloin. Don't miss the pan-seared calamari or the baked spinach salad, which are reasons enough to visit.

LODGING   For an incredible experience, book a *casita* at the **Inn at Dos Brisas** (9400 Champion Dr.; 979-277-7750; www.dosbrisas.com), a 300-acre luxury ranch that features an incredible restaurant, organic farm, and full range of activities such as fishing, mountain biking, and hiking. Accommodations are set up as little houses featuring leather duvet covers, 1,200-thread-count sheets, fully stocked refrigerators, a stocked amenities closet, a complimentary bottle of champagne upon arrival, and use of a personal golf cart. Trust me—once you get here, you won't want to be anywhere else.

If I'm wrong, however, another lodging option is **Mariposa Ranch Bed and Breakfast** (8904 Mariposa Lane; 979-836-4737; www.mariposaranch.com), a working ranch that aims to offer "casual elegance" to its guests through its well-appointed houses, cabins, and cottages.

DAY 2/MORNING

BREAKFAST Start your second day in the country off right at the **Inn at Dos Brisas restaurant**, (9400 Champion Dr.; 979-277-7750; www.dosbrisas.com), which serves lunch Sat from 11 a.m. to 2 p.m. and brunch Sun from 11 a.m. to 2 p.m. Prefer to eat in private? Individual meals can be prepared for guests to enjoy as a picnic or inside their private casita. Brunch offerings include house-made ricotta gnocchi, tempura soft-shell crab, and ginger spice cake with cinnamon crème anglaise and carrot ginger sorbet.

Want something on the go? Try the **Funky Art Café & Coffee Bar** (202 W. Commerce St.; 979-836-5220; www.funkyartcafe.com), a funky—yes, it's actually funky—little cafe featuring a full coffee bar as well as soups, salads, sandwiches, and wraps. Open Mon through Fri from 11 a.m. to 2 p.m. and Sat from 11 a.m. to 3 p.m.

From the inn, go east on Champion Drive to FM 1155 and go right, then take that to US 290 and go west. Go right on E. Mulberry Street/TX 125 Loop, then right on N. Main Street until you see the **Burton Cotton Gin & Museum** (307 N. Main St. in Burton; 979-289-3378; www.cottonginmuseum.org). Home of the oldest operating cotton gin in America, this museum offers an interesting and interactive—guests may even pick cotton during their tour—look at the history of the cotton industry in Texas. The museum is open Tues through Sat from 10 a.m. to 4 p.m., and admission is free. Guided tours are offered daily at 10 a.m. and 2 p.m. for a fee of $6 for adults, $4 for students, and free for children under 5. Two other places also worth a quick visit in Burton are the **Burton Depot,** a historic train depot that served as a terminal on the Houston and

Texas Central Railroad in 1870, and the **Mt. Zion Cemetery and Historic Chapel.** For more information, visit http://burtonheritage society.org.

LUNCH Now, go southeast on N. Main Street/TX 125, turn left on E. Mulberry Street, then go right on US 290 west. Take that to TX 237 south, go left on Main Street and stop once you reach **Royer's Round Top Café** (105 Main St. in Round Top; 979-249-3611; www.royersroundtopcafe.com), a fantastic little cafe that features a wide selection of food including grilled fresh Gulf snapper, grilled rack of lamb, beef tenderloin, and shrimp-stuffed grilled quail. Sound fancy? It's not. The place is über-casual: As long as you're wearing a shirt, shoes, and pants, you're good to go. Warning: The place is small—about forty seats—but the lines move quick. Still full from your late breakfast? At least get a slice of Royer's famous pie. Selections include Bud's butterscotch chip pie, Ann's pecan pie, and a rotating variety of fruit pie. Royer's is open Thurs through Sat from 11 a.m. to 9 p.m. and Sun from 11 a.m. to 3 p.m.

AFTERNOON

Next, go northwest on Main Street to N. Washington Street/TX 237 and go left. TX 237 becomes TX 159. Continue on until you reach E. Travis Street and go left onto S. Jefferson Street/US 77. Go right on Summit Street/US 90, left on TX 222 Spur, and right on N. Main Street until you reach **Sengelmann Hall** (531 N. Main St. in Schulenburg; http://sengelmannhall.com), a fully restored 1890s Texas dance hall with a restaurant, saloon, and biergarten. Bring your boots and float across the longleaf pine floor, sip a cold beverage at a picnic table outside, or listen for the ghosts that allegedly haunt the hall. Check the website for restaurant and dance hall hours, which are subject to change.

There's More . . . .

History. Brenham Antique Carousel. A classic carousel believed to have been carved by Charles Dare between 1867 and 1901. Located in Brenham's Fireman's Park; (979) 337-7250; www.ci .brenham.tx.us/parks/carousel.cfm.

Brenham Heritage Museum. Offers insight into the interesting history of the region. 105 S. Market St.; (979) 830-8445; www .brenhamheritagemuseum.org.

Chappell Hill Historic District. Located in the nearby town of Chappell Hill, this district features unique shops and restaurants. Along Main Street in Chappell Hill; www.chappellhilltx.com.

Heritage Home Tours. Visit homes from the 1800s featuring many classic furnishings. 2203 Century Circle; (979) 836-1690; www.giddingsstonemansion.com.

Seward Plantation. Beautiful plantation built in the 1850s. FM 390 in Independence; (979) 830-5388.

Museum. Sterling McCall Cadillac Museum. Features historic information and actual Cadillac models that were made starting in 1904. TX 237 in Warrenton; (979) 249-5089; www.sterlingmccall museum.org.

Wildlife. Americana Alpacas. A family-owned alpaca ranch that welcomes visitors in Navasota. Call to set up a tour; (936) 870-3887; www.americanaalpacas.com.

Nueces Canyon Equestrian Center & Resort. A working ranch offering lodging and horse-related activities. 9501 US 290 west; (979) 289-5600; www.nuecescanyon.com.

Special Events & Festivals . . . .

APRIL

Cotton Gin Festival, Burton. Celebrates keeping the history and heritage of cotton alive. (979) 289-3378; www.cottonginmuseum .org/Festivals.htm.

Official Bluebonnet Festival of Texas, Chappell Hill. A celebration of the state's favorite flower. Held along Chappell Hill's Main Street; www.chappellhillmuseum.org/festivals.htm.

Round Top Spring Antiques Fair, Round Top. Twice yearly fair (the other takes place in fall) that features a huge offering of antiques. Held at various dealers in Round Top; (512) 237-4747; www .roundtoptexasantiques.com.

MAY

Fayetteville Chamber Music Festival, Fayetteville. Features chamber music concerts by the best musicians in the region. Held at the square in downtown Fayetteville; (979) 249-5035; www.fayette villemusic.org.

Maifest, Brenham. German heritage festival featuring music, food, beer, and more. Held at Fireman's Park; (979) 830-5393; www .maifest.org.

JUNE

Shakespeare at Winedale, Winedale. A University of Texas program in which students study and perform plays in a converted nineteenth-century barn that also serves as a theater; www.utexas.edu/cola /progs/winedale.

AUGUST
Chappell Hill Lavender Festival, Chappell Hill. A celebration of lavender at multiple local venues; www.chappellhilllavender.com.

Other Recommended Restaurants & Lodgings . . . . .

BRENHAM
Big Daddy's BBQ, 1309 Prairie Lea St. in Brenham; (979) 830-1619. Amazing barbecue served from inside a gas station.

Brazos Bed & Breakfast, 20251 Pickens Rd.; (936) 878-2230; www.brazosbedandbreakfast.com. Peaceful, centrally located B&B.

Brenham Olde Towne Bakery, 301 S. Charles St. in Brenham; (979) 836-2253. Fantastic coffee and baked goods.

Capital Grille, 107 West Commerce St.; (979) 251-7800. Quiet, romantic Italian restaurant.

Red Room Restaurant, 1503 US 290 east in Brenham; (979) 251-7791. Breakfast and lunch spot with great steak, sandwiches, and soups.

Tara Farmers B&B, 2191 FM 109 in Brenham; (979) 836-7098; www.tarafarmsbrenham.com. A beautiful retreat near major attractions.

BURTON
Pig & Whistle, 12607 W. Washington St. in Burton; (979) 289-2319; www.pigandwhistleofburtontexas.com. Great pub and grill with outside seating.

Toad Hollow Icehouse, 10091 Longpoint Rd. in Burton; (979) 289-2131. Laid-back beer joint.

WASHINGTON
R Place at Washington-on-the-Brazos, 23254 FM 1155 in Washington; (936) 878-1925; www.rplacetexas.com. Fun little barbecue joint with Blue Bell ice cream and beer.

For More Information . . . .

Downtown Brenham; www.downtownbrenham.com.

City of Brenham; www.ci.brenham.tx.us.

General Washington County info; www.co.washington.tx.us.

Washington County Chamber of Commerce; www.brenhamtexas.com.

WESTBOUND ESCAPE *Two*
Austin
KEEPING IT WEIRD IN THE CAPITAL CITY / 2 NIGHTS

- Live music
- Outdoor adventures
- State capitol
- Nightlife
- Quirky culture

When you visit a place known for live music, a booming nightlife, incredible outdoor offerings, and a penchant for all things quirky (the unofficial city motto is "Keep Austin Weird," which locals have embraced wholeheartedly) you know you're going to have an entertaining weekend.

The city was originally founded as the town of Waterloo in 1837 and named for Stephen F. Austin, "the father of Texas," who negotiated a boundary treaty with the local Native American residents near Treaty Oak. For years Austin was a quiet hippie community sitting in the shadows of larger cities such as Dallas and San Antonio. But now it has blossomed into one of the must-see destinations in the state. Known as the "live music capital of the world," Austin regularly draws visitors from around the globe, including celebrities who come for gigs, movie shoots, or major festivals and decide they'd like to stay awhile.

This melting pot for techies, movie buffs, and musicians is sure to satisfy any of your curiosities—artistic or otherwise.

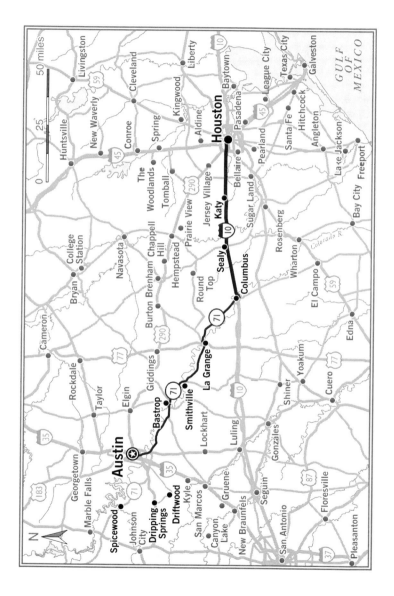

DAY 1/MORNING

From Houston, take I-10 west to TX 71 west, and you'll be in Austin in less than three hours.

BREAKFAST   On your way, stop in La Grange, which is about halfway through the trip, and pick up some kolaches at **Weikel's Bakery** (2247 W. TX 71; 979-968-9413; www.weikels.com). Don't let its unassuming spot inside a Shell gas station fool you—this place is known for having some of the best Czech pastries in the state. For sweet kolaches, try the cheese or apple filled; for savory, go for sausage and cheese.

Then, start your Austin weekend by zipping high above the trees at **Cypress Valley Canopy Tours** (223 Paleface Ranch Rd. off TX 71 in Spicewood; 512-264-8880; www.cypressvalleycanopytours .com), which offers zip-line tours of the lush Texas Hill Country. Visitors will soar across cable lines as long as 350 feet and land on platforms placed up to 40 feet high in the trees. It's an exhilarating experience for anyone who'd like to see the greens and browns of the Austin area from a bird's-eye view. Individual tours are $65 and are offered from 9 a.m. to dusk Mon through Fri and noon to dusk Sun from Memorial Day to Labor Day. No children under 10 are permitted, and children 10–17 must be accompanied by an adult. During spring and fall, call for the schedule. The park is closed Mon.

Now that you've worked up a sweat, make the short drive east on TX 71 to **Hamilton Pool** (24300 Hamilton Pool Rd. in Dripping Springs; 512-264-2740; www.co.travis.tx.us/tnr/parks/ hamilton_pool.asp), a 232-acre swimming hole that features a plunging waterfall surrounded by a grotto, canyon, and a multitude of plants and wildlife. Bring walking shoes—the hike into the pool is about 0.25 mile on sometimes rocky terrain. Once you arrive at the water, however, expect a beautiful oasis like something out of a movie. Open daily 9 a.m. to 6 p.m. Early arrival is recommended, as the parking lot frequently reaches capacity in the morning hours. Admission is $10 per vehicle, cash or check only. Call ahead to make sure the pool is open for swimming, as heavy rains can impact the bacteria levels in the water and cause temporary closures.

LUNCH When it comes to Texas barbecue, no place is more legendary—or more delicious—than **The Salt Lick** (18300 FM 1826 in Driftwood; 512-858-4959; www.saltlickbbq.com). From Hamilton Pool Road, go left on Ranch Road 12, then left on FM 50 to FM 1826. The restaurant will be on your left. Having smoked meats in the same location since 1967, the Salt Lick's food is known for its mouthwatering perfection, from fall-apart-in-your mouth brisket to succulent pork ribs to tangy potato salad. An Austin institution, the Salt Lick now has three area locations, but the Driftwood location, the original, is a must-see for any uninitiated visitor. Hit the ATM before you go, though, because it's cash only here, and BYOB.

AFTERNOON

After lunch, take FM 1826 west to TX 71 until you see the **South Congress Avenue** exit. Go left and park somewhere between the 1000 and 1600 blocks. Packed with cool boutiques, unique restaurants, antiques stores, folk art shops, and laid-back watering holes, this walkable shopping and entertainment corridor, nicknamed SoCo, will keep you entertained for most of the afternoon.

If you're a clothes fanatic, check out **Blackmail** (1202 S. Congress; 512-326-7670; www.blackmailboutique.com), where almost every item in the store, from dresses to skirts to T-shirts, is—you guessed it—black. Don't miss the fantastic collection of vintage cowboy boots in the back of the store.

Like jewelry? Head to **Lucy in Disguise With Diamonds and Electric Ladyland** (1506 S. Congress; 512-444-2002; www.lucy

indisguise.com), a costume shop known for fabulous, and fabulously cheap, costume jewelry. Accessories such as belt buckles, earrings, watches, and necklaces start at 99 cents. Going to a costume party? You're in luck. Costumes here range from the funny (i.e., a chicken with its head cut off) to the funky (i.e., disco diva) to the fabulous (i.e., rainbow Cher).

If you want a one-of-a-kind souvenir, you can't miss **Parts and Labour** (1117 S. Congress; 512-326-1648; www.partsandlabour .com), which features "functional artwork" such as jewelry, clothing, and accessories created by Texas artists. On any given day, expect pens made from bullets, hand-crocheted monster stuffed animals, and Dr Pepper bud vases, for example.

And if you want something goofy, try **Monkey See, Monkey Do!** (1712 S. Congress; 512-443-4999; www.monkeyseeonline.com), where kids (and kids at heart) congregate to get their fix of items such as giant robots, wind-up teeth, Magic 8 balls, sushi air fresheners, and ironic magnets.

Should you need an energy boost during all that shopping, stop by **Hey Cupcake!** (1600 S. Congress; 512-476-2253; www.heycup cakeaustin.com), where chocolate, vanilla, red velvet, and carrot cake creations come served up fresh from the window of a vintage Airstream trailer. Get there early, though. Once they run out of cupcakes, they close down for the day. Not in the mood for cupcakes? Stop by one of the other food trailers located in the same lot.

Shopped out? Take a fifteen-minute walk (or two-minute drive) down S. Congress to the **Congress Avenue Bridge** (100 Congress Ave.), where 1.5 million Mexican free-tail bats (the country's largest urban bat colony) emerge between mid-Mar and Nov around dusk to search for food, blanketing the sky in black. Even if it doesn't sound all that exciting to you, you've got to go at least once. It's an Austin tradition. For a special experience, rent a kayak or canoe and watch the scene from the water. Or if you want something more structured, sign up for the sunset cruise on the **Lonestar Riverboat** (512-327-1388; www.lonestarriverboat.com), an electric-powered paddle wheeler that offers views of this nightly event.

DINNER   Head back down South Congress to the 1400 block to end your own search for food at **Perla's Seafood and Oyster Bar** (1400 S. Congress, 512-291-7300, www.perlasaustin.com), where fresh oysters and fish are flown in daily from both coasts and perfectly made cocktails are the order of the day. Don't miss the cornmeal fried Gulf oysters or delightful homemade margarita. The restaurant offers a happy hour daily from 3 to 6 p.m. and a weekend brunch.

NIGHTLIFE   Wrap up your evening across the street at the **Continental Club** (1315 S. Congress; 512-441-0202; www.continentalclub.com), which has been one of Austin's best, and most-loved, music venues since 1957. Performers have included Stevie Ray Vaughan, Joe Ely, Butthole Surfers, Kinky Friedman, and Charlie Sexton. Regardless of the artist, the mix of blues, folk, country, and soul performed here will have your toes tapping. Cover varies depending on the artist. Call ahead to check.

LODGING   If you're going to be spending so much time in the heart of the city, it's only smart to pick a hotel that's centrally located. **Hotel San Jose** (1316 S. Congress; 512-444-7322; www.sanjosehotel.com) is an Austin treasure with a beautiful courtyard, gorgeous European-style rooms, and a friendly yet hip vibe. Don't miss having a cocktail—frequently made with local ingredients—in the garden courtyard. Rates start around $95 a night.

Traveling with the family? Look just a block down to the **Austin Motel** (1220 S. Congress; 512-441-1157; www.austinmotel.com), where the forty-one rooms and sparkling 1950s-style pool will keep your entire clan happy. Room decor varies depending on the room. Examples include a "polka-dot surprise" with turquoise and yellow polka-dot decor; the art-inspired "Monet honeymoon"; and the relaxing "Zen." Don't mind the questionable-looking sign out front: It's completely family-friendly. Rates start around $100.

DAY 2/MORNING

BREAKFAST The sign on the door may read, "Sorry, we're open," but you won't be disappointed with breakfast at **Magnolia Cafe** (1920 S. Congress; 512-445-0000; www.themagnoliacafe.com). Serving breakfast twenty-four hours a day, Magnolia dishes up some of the best omelets, breakfast tacos, and pancakes in town. Don't miss the incredible gingerbread short stack, the "Love migas," or the queso omelet. In more of a lunch mood? You're in luck, as the lunch offerings are just as delicious as the breakfast ones. Favorite items include the hummus and tabouli plate, the magna cristo (turkey, ham, bacon, Swiss cheese, avocado, and tomato on grilled Italian white bread), and the voodoo blue cheese burger.

Next, go north on S. Congress Avenue to Cesar Chavez and go right until you reach the Camacho Center for a stand-up paddle boarding lesson with **The Expedition School** (34 Robert Martinez Jr. St.; 512-626-6282; www.expeditionschool.org). Mixing elements of surfing and kayaking, stand-up paddle boarding has taken hold in Austin because it involves a strong core workout while giving participants a surface view of one of the most-loved parts of the city—**Lady Bird Lake**. The business is owned by surfer–mountain climber–extreme hiker Kimery Duda, who will show you the ropes in a warm, encouraging manner. Go early in the morning for a remarkably serene view of town.

Following your lesson, take Cesar Chavez Street to I-35 north and exit 235A. Turn left on 15th Street, then right on Congress, and park at **The Bob Bullock Texas State History Museum** (1800 N. Congress; 512-936-8746; www.thestoryoftexas.com). The three floors in this museum use interactive exhibits, a special effects show, and an IMAX theater to tell the "story of Texas." Exhibits include Encounters of the Land, which details the first meetings of Native Americans and European explorers; Creating Opportunity, which covers the history and importance of ranching in Texas; and

Building the Lone Star Identity, which discusses the Texas Revolution. Open Mon through Sat from 9 a.m. to 6 p.m. and Sun from noon to 6 p.m. Admission is $7 for adults, $4 for youths ages 5–18, and free for children under 5. IMAX and theater tickets include additional fees.

LUNCH No trip to Austin is complete without a Tex-Mex lunch, and no place is better to get one than **El Arroyo** (1616 W. 5th St.; 512-478-2577; www .ditch.com). Known for the funny messages on the signboard out front and for delicious margaritas, queso, and enchiladas, El Arroyo is the place to load up for your afternoon of sightseeing. It's even mentioned in a popular Pat Green song ("Let's have some tacos and beer down at El Arroyo..."). Don't miss the fresh spinach con queso, Mexican crab rolls, sour cream chicken enchiladas, or the daily drink specials, such as $1 Tecates all day Mon and $1 margaritas from 2 to 6 p.m. Thurs. Entrees run about $10.

AFTERNOON

Full? Go left on W. 5th Street until you hit Lamar Boulevard and go right. From there, take a right on Barton Springs Road and follow that until you see the **Zilker Botanical Gardens** (2220 Barton Springs Rd.; 512-477-8672; www.zilkergarden.org) on your right. With thirty-one acres featuring a cactus and succulent garden, a Japanese garden, a butterfly trail, and a pioneer village, it's a great place to learn about the flora and fauna of Austin—and a great spot for photo opportunities. Open 7 a.m. to 5:30 p.m. Admission is generally free except for special events. Parking is free on weekdays and $3 per car on weekends.

Once you leave the gardens, go left on Barton Springs Road and take a right into **Zilker Park** (2100 Barton Springs Rd.; 512-974-6700; www.ci.austin.tx.us/zilker), a 351-acre metropolitan park that includes a nine-hole Frisbee golf course, kayak and canoe rentals along Lady Bird Lake, hike and bike trails, picnic areas, a miniature train that circles the park, a playground, and the spring-fed **Barton Springs Pool,** an Austin institution. The park is open daily from 5 a.m. to 10 p.m. and admission is free, but fees are frequently charged for parking and special events. Admission to Barton Springs Pool is $3 for adults, $2 for ages 12–17, and $1 for seniors and children under 12.

After you leave the park, head east on Barton Springs Road and take your first right, then your first left into **Umlauf Sculpture Garden** (605 Robert E. Lee Rd.; 512-445-5582; www.umlauf sculpture.org). Featuring the creations of Charles Umlauf and other contemporary sculptors, the garden is a cool place to spend an hour or so. Open Wed through Fri from 10 a.m. to 4:30 p.m. and Sat and Sun from 1 to 4:30 p.m. Closed Mon and Tues. Admission is $3.50 for adults, $2.50 for seniors, $1 for students, and free for children 6 and under.

DINNER After your day of sightseeing, go east on Barton Springs Road and stop at **Shady Grove** (1624 Barton Springs Rd.; 512-474-9991; www.the shadygrove.com). Grab a seat outside under one of the towering leafy trees, order a signature "Shady Thang" (their twist on a frozen margarita) and watch the incredible array of people who wander through. In terms of food, you can't miss with the Hippie Chick sandwich, Tortilla-Fried Queso Catfish, chiliburger, or Frito pie. Bands play on Thurs in spring and fall. Entrees start around $8.

NIGHTLIFE Since no visit to Austin would be complete without a trip to the raucous insanity that is the **6th Street nightlife district** (located on 6th between Congress Avenue and I-35), head east on Barton Springs Road, and go left on Congress Avenue until you hit 6th Street. Park, then walk to the entertainment district, which is filled with every kind of libation for every kind of person imaginable. One of the most popular bars on the strip is **The Library Bar** (407 E. 6th St.; 512-236-0662;

www.librarybars.com), where Long Island iced teas and '90s alt-rock are the order of the day. If you want something a little less frat-tastic, try **The Jackalope** (404 E. 6th St.; 512-469-5801; www.jackalopebar.com), which is known for its "dive bar" vibe, solid beer selection, and surprisingly decent food. Want to watch the action without the worry of being featured in an upcoming episode of the *Real World*? Grab a seat at the hip upstairs patio at the **Iron Cactus** (606 Trinity St.; 512-472-9240; www .ironcactus.com) and watch the debauchery ensue from up above it all.

DAY 3/MORNING

BREAKFAST   Start with coffee and breakfast tacos at **Jo's** (1300 S. Congress Ave.; 512-444-3800; www.joscoffee.com), an outdoor coffee shop nestled between Hotel San Jose and the Austin Motel. Probably the most popular spot for people-watching in Austin, this tiny shop is packed with locals and visitors on weekend mornings. But even if you have to wait, it's worth it, as the coffee is flavorful, the pastries are tender, and the Wi-Fi is strong.

Next, go north on Congress Avenue and then turn left on W. Riverside Drive. Next, turn right onto Lamar Boulevard until you reach the **flagship Whole Foods Market** (525 N. Lamar Blvd.; 512-476-1206; www.wholefoodsmarket.com). This store may now be available in cities around the country, but it was founded in Austin and the flagship store is unlike any other store you've ever been to. This 80,000-square-foot structure includes a sprawling patio, ecofriendly product demonstrations, beer tastings, and a culinary center with cooking classes and catering options. Examples of some recent cooking classes include Kitchen Fundamentals: Fish Cookery; Crazy for Coconuts; Teen Cooking Camp; and a Beer and Cheese Tasting.

While you're in the area, visit some of the nearby shops, which include upscale boutique **By George** (524 N. Lamar Blvd.;

877-472-5951; www.bygeorgeaustin.com), **Waterloo Records and Video** (600 N. Lamar Blvd.; 512-474-2500; www.waterloorecords .com), and **Amy's Ice Cream** (1012 W. 6th St.; 512-480-0673; www.amysicecreams.com).

LUNCH Before you head home, walk a few blocks down to **Opal Divine's Freehouse** (700 W. 6th St.; 512-477-3308; www.opaldivines.com), a restaurant-bar with a huge patio, fantastic drinks, and a wonderful pub-grub-meets-American-classics menu. This is a perfect place to go on a casual date or meet up with a group of friends. The battered mushrooms, divine quesadilla (spinach, mushroom, roasted red peppers, and feta cheese on an onion tortilla), and the hippie Benedict (tomato and avocado slices with sprouts, covered in hollandaise sauce) are signature items. The hippie Benedict is only served during brunch, which is offered from 10 a.m. to 3 p.m. on weekends.

There's More . . . .

Campus. **University of Texas Campus.** Highlights include the LBJ Library, the Blanton Museum of Art, and the UT Tower. Walking tours are available Mon through Sat at the Main Building near the Tower. Campus is bordered by Guadalupe, MLK, Red River, and Dean Keeton Streets; (512) 471-1988; www.utexas.edu.

Nature. **Lady Bird Johnson Wildflower Center.** Offers a mosaic of spectacular native flowers dedicated to the former First Lady at 4801 La Crosse Ave.; (512) 232-0100; www.wildflower.org.

Outdoors. **Deep Eddy.** Spring-fed pool near Lady Bird Lake. 401 Deep Eddy Dr.; (512) 472-8546; www.deepeddy.org.

Lady Bird Lake Hike and Bike Trail. Ten miles of stunning trails set on the lake in the center of the city; (512) 974-2000; www.ci .austin.tx.us.

History. **Texas Capitol.** A trip to Austin isn't complete without a stop at the state capitol at 112 E. 11th St.; (512) 305-8400; www.tspb .state.tx.us.

Special Events & Festivals . . . .

If you have some flexibility, consider timing your Austin jaunt to coincide with one of its many festivals. Here are a few favorites:

MARCH
SXSW. Held every Mar to coincide with spring break, this film, music, and interactive festival draws artists from around the globe. It's a good place to discover rising—or see established—talent; www.sxsw.com.

APRIL
Eeyore's Birthday Party. Perhaps the most bizarre yet entertaining festival in the city, the annual Eeyore's Birthday Party offers a vibrant ode to that oh-so-melancholy donkey. Held every Apr in Pease Park, 1100 Kingsbury St., the party has grown to include a gigantic drum circle, dancers, face-painting, and other family-friendly activities; www.eeyores.com.

MAY
Pecan Street Festival. This Austin tradition features arts and crafts from more than 250 artisans hawking everything from hammocks to artwork to turkey legs. Held along downtown's famous 6th Street district, the festival, which is also held in Sept, is a great way for visitors to see the city; www.oldpecanstreetfestival.com.

OCTOBER
Austin City Limits Festival. Bringing together the best bands from around the world, ACL has become one of the premiere music

festivals in the country. Past performers have included Bob Dylan, Joss Stone, Kings of Leon, The Walkmen, and Foo Fighters. One-day and three-day passes are available; www.aclfestival.com.

Other Recommended Restaurants & Lodgings . . . . .

24 Diner, 600 N. Lamar Blvd.; (512) 472-5400; www.24diner .com. This relatively new eatery offers delicious "chef inspired comfort food."

Antone's, 213 W. 5th St.; (512) 320-8424; www.antones.net. The area's best bluegrass, folk, funk, and blues.

Austin Java Company, multiple Austin locations; www.austinjava .com. Sandwiches, salads, and yes, lots of java.

The Driskill Hotel, 604 Brazos St.; (800) 252-9367; www.driskill hotel.com. Beautiful, historic hotel in the heart of downtown.

Emo's, 603 Red River; (512) 505-8541; www.emosaustin.com. Alternative lounge with live music.

Ginny's Little Longhorn, 5434 Burnet Rd.; (512) 458-1813; www .myspace.com/littlelonghornsaloon. A true Texas dive bar. Don't miss the "special" bingo on Sun.

Hotel Saint Cecilia, 112 Academy Dr.; (512) 852-2400; www .hotelsaintcecilia.com. Hip, music-centric spot run by the same folks as Hotel San Jose.

Hudson's on the Bend, 3509 Ranch Rd. 620 N; (512) 266-1369; www.hudsonsonthebend.com. Come here for a rustic, laid-back dinner.

InterContinental Stephen F. Austin Hotel, 701 Congress Ave.; (512) 457-8800; www.austin.intercontinental.com. Upscale lodging near the Texas Capitol.

Kimber Modern, 110 The Circle; (512) 912-1046; www.kimber modern.com. Boutique hotel with a unique self-service model.

Moonshine, 303 Red River St.; (512) 236-9599; www.moonshine grill.com. Bar and grill with an amazing Sunday brunch.

The Parish, 214-C E. 6th St.; (512) 473-8381; www.theparish austin.com. Intimate indoor venue for local and touring acts.

Radisson Hotel & Suites, 111 E. Cesar Chavez St.; (512) 478-9611; www.radisson.com. Affordable hotel with impressive views of Lady Bird Lake.

Stubb's, 801 Red River; (512) 480-8341; www.stubbsaustin.com. Major and local acts in a terrific outdoor setting.

Trudy's, multiple Austin locations; (512) 477-2935; www.trudys.com. Delicious Tex-Mex and drinks.

Uchi, 801 S. Lamar Blvd.; (512) 916-4808; www.uchiaustin.com. The best sushi in town, hands down.

For More Information . . . .

Austin Chamber of Commerce, 210 Barton Springs Rd., Suite 400; (512) 478-9383; www.austinchamber.com.

Austin Convention & Visitors Bureau, 301 Congress Ave., Ste. 200; (800) 926-2282; www.austintexas.org.

Austin 360. Entertainment and events listings all around Austin; www.austin360.com.

Travis County official website; www.co.travis.tx.us.

WESTBOUND ESCAPE *Three*

Hill Country One—Fredericksburg Area

DRINKING UP THE TEXAS HILL COUNTRY / 2 NIGHTS

Nestled in the heart of the Texas Hill Country, the Fredericksburg area epitomizes all of the things that someone seeks in a weekend getaway. From incredible hiking opportunities and swimming holes to live music and wine tasting, there's a little something for everyone.

- Wine tasting
- Outdoor activities
- Swimming holes
- Luckenbach
- Laid-back lifestyle

If Texas had a Napa Valley, it would be this little enclave, which is home to a half-dozen wineries stomping out some of the best U.S.-made wine anywhere. Designate a driver and dedicate at least an afternoon to touring them—you won't regret it.

No matter what time of year you go, you're sure to enjoy the endless sunshine, rolling hills, and music that seems to radiate from every corner.

DAY 1/MORNING

From Houston, take I-10 west toward San Antonio, then merge onto TX 71 west toward La Grange/Austin. That turns into US 290 west.

BREAKFAST Once you reach US 290 west, stop at **Flores Breakfast Tacos** (920 US 290 west before Might Tiger Lane in Dripping Springs; 512-858-9346), which is one of the best places in the area to grab a breakfast taco. The tortillas are warm, the salsas are tangy, and the ingredients are fresh—yum. Flavor combinations are basic but delicious, such as potato and egg, chorizo and potato, and bacon and egg. Even better? They're only about $1.

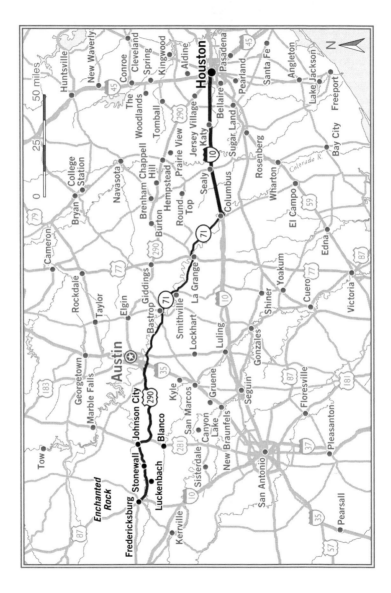

Next, go west on US 290 to US 281 and go north. After about 4 miles, you will see Zoo Trail and go right to **Exotic Resort Zoo** (235 Zoo Trail in Johnson City; 830-868-4357; www.zooexotics .com), which is home to more than 500 animals and eighty different species. As you tour the sprawling park, you're likely to see anything from zebras to camels to kangaroos to giraffes to bison. Tours cost $11.95 for adults, $9.95 for children 2–12, and $10.95 for seniors and run from 9 a.m. to 6 p.m. daily. Feed for the animals is available in the gift shop for an additional fee. Cabins are also available for guests who want to stay overnight.

After the zoo, head back to US 281 and go left. Follow that to Main Street and go right, then go left on Park Road 23 and end at **Blanco State Park** (Park Road 23 in Blanco; 830-833-4333; www.tpwd.state.tx.us). This park has a variety of features including camping, fishing, picnicking, hiking, and kayaking, but the biggest draw here is the swimming. Located on a beautiful rushing dam, the park is a fun place for all ages. Youngsters will enjoy walking across the top of the dam as the water flows over their toes, and adults will like swimming at the bottom of the dam, where waves crash down like a waterfall. It's also extremely picturesque, with the trees reflecting perfectly off the blue-green water. Bring a camera— you won't want to miss a thing.

LUNCH Once you've air dried, go north on Park Road 23 to Main Street and go left, then go right on 4th Street to **Riley's B-B-Q** (318 4th St. in Blanco; 830-833-4166; www.rileysbarbq.com), which has been open since 2003 and serves up classics such as pork ribs, turkey breast, sausage, chicken, and brisket that's slow cooked for sixteen hours before it hits your plate. The sides are almost as varied, with options such as deviled eggs, potato salad, french fries, marinated onions, and more. Don't miss the fried chicken and fried okra with sweet tea. Open Mon through Sat from 11 a.m. to 8 p.m. and Sun from 11 a.m. to 6 p.m.

In the mood for dessert? Head next door to the **Blanco Bowling Club Café** (310 4th St.; 830-833-4416), home to some of the best, and biggest, pies around. Don't miss the pecan, apple, or meringue pies, which are so huge that they tower off the table. Go early, though—the pies have a tendency to sell out.

Want something more traditional? Try **Silver K** (209 E. Main St. in Johnson City; 830-868-2911; www.silverkcafe.com), which serves up Southern comfort food, soups, and sandwiches daily starting at 11 a.m.

AFTERNOON

From US 290 west, exit on Park Road 52 to **Lyndon B. Johnson State Park & Historic Site** (Park Road 52 in Stonewall; 830-644-2478; www.tpwd.state.tx.us), where visitors can swim, picnic, fish, and view wildlife such as buffalo, longhorns, and white-tailed deer. In the visitor center, a variety of memorabilia from the president's time in office is displayed. Bus tours of the LBJ Ranch leave from the visitor center and include the one-room Junction School, which 4-year-old LBJ attended in 1912; the Johnson family cemetery, where he is buried; and the still-in-operation LBJ Ranch. The park also houses the Sauer-Beckmann Farmstead, a living history farm that functions as though it were 1918. No entrance fee is charged at the park, but there may be certain activity fees. Call ahead for hours and cost.

Now, go back on US 290 west, take a left at S. Ranch Road 1623, go straight for 1.5 miles, and turn right on Upper Albert Road to start your tour of the **Texas Wine Trail** at **Pedernales Cellars** (2916 Upper Albert Rd. in Stonewall; 830-644-2037; www.pedernalescellars.com). This seventeen-acre vineyard and 15,000-square-foot winemaking facility turns out varietals such as tempranillo, monastrell, cabernet sauvignon, and merlot. The tasting room is open Mon through Thurs from 10 a.m. to 5 p.m.,

Fri and Sat from 10 a.m. to 6 p.m., and Sun from noon to 6 p.m., and guests are welcome to roam the vineyards and enjoy the view as long as they'd like. The tasting free is $12.95 a person, which includes nine wines and a logo wine glass. Private tours are also available.

Next, hop back on US 290 west and exit at Jenschke Lane; turn right at Becker Farms Road to reach **Becker Vineyards** (464 Becker Farms Rd. in Stonewall; 830-644-2681; www.beckervineyards .com). This vineyard, which was created in 1992, includes forty-six acres of vines that produce syrah, sauvignon blanc, malbec, cabernet sauvignon, and merlot, among others. The 10,040-square-foot winery, which is located in a nineteenth-century barn, is open Mon through Thurs from 10 a.m. to 5 p.m., Fri and Sat from 10 a.m. to 6 p.m., and Sun from noon to 6 p.m. The cost is $10 for six tastings. When you're finished, take the time to tour the property, which is surrounded by peach orchards, native wildflowers, lavender, and grazing quarter horses.

Now, head back to US 290 west and stop when you see the rock bell tower of **Grape Creek Vineyards** (10587 E. US 290 in Fredericksburg; 830-644-2710; www.grapecreek.com), which calls itself the "Tuscany in Texas." An expansive winery featuring wide blocks of vines, an upgraded winemaking facility, and a tasting room with a 40-foot bar, Grape Creek is a must-see on your wine tasting route. Tastings cost $10 and include six wines and a Grape Creek wine glass; the fee is refunded with a three-bottle purchase. Open Mon through Fri from 11 a.m. to 6 p.m., Sat from 10 a.m. to 6 p.m.; and Sun from 11 a.m. to 5 p.m.

Finally, wrap up your wine tour by heading back to US 290 west and following that until you hit W. Main Street in Fredericksburg and see the **Fredericksburg Winery** (247 W. Main St.; 830-990-8747; www.fbgwinery.com). This 10,600-square-foot facility in the heart of downtown was named one of the top three wine producers in Texas by *USA Today*. The winery is open Mon through Thurs from 10 a.m. to 5:30 p.m., Fri and Sat from 10 a.m. to 7:30 p.m., and Sun from noon to 5:30 p.m. Hours are subject to change, however, so call ahead to confirm.

Should you find yourself with extra time for wine tasting, there are plenty of other recommended wineries. They include **Fall Creek Vineyards** (1820 CR 222 in Tow; 325-379-5361), **Sister Creek Vineyards** (1142 Sisterdale Rd. in Sisterdale; 830-324-6704; www .sistercreekvineyards.com), and **Woodrose Winery** (662 Woodrose Lane in Stonewall; 830-644-2539; www.woodrosewinery.com).

DINNER After the day you've had, you're going to need a good dinner, so follow E. Main Street to the **The Auslander Restaurant and Biergarten** (323 E. Main St.; 830-997-7714; www.theauslander.com), where the authentic German food will fill you up in a jiffy. Menu items include Bavarian potato skins (skins filled with German sausage, sauerkraut, cabbage, and smothered in melted Swiss), a schnitzel burger, flame-grilled rib eye, and, of course, bratwurst with sauerkraut. Don't miss the delicious beer-battered mushrooms or the fantastic Reuben. Live music, beer, and wine—should you want to order a glass of one you tried earlier in the day—are also available. Open daily from 11 a.m. to 9 p.m.; the bar is open 11 a.m. to midnight daily except Wed.

In the mood for something a little more upscale? Try **The Nest** (607 S. Washington St.; 830-990-8383; www.thenestrestaurant.com), a bistro featuring seafood, steaks, and incredible desserts. Entrees include items such as broiled semiboneless quail stuffed with bacon, spinach, goat cheese, and sun-dried tomatoes on green chile polenta with a port demi-glace; pan-seared sea scallops with chipotle lime hollandaise and sautéed spinach and turnip mashed potatoes; and roasted New Zealand rack of lamb with a pecan pesto and stone ground mustard demi-glace.

NIGHTLIFE After dinner, it's time to visit a local institution. Take Main Street/US 290 east to RR 1376 and go right, then take a right onto Luckenbach

Town Loop and end at **Luckenbach** (412 Luckenbach Town Loop; 830-997-3224; www.luckenbachtexas.com). This small Texas town is known as a hub for live music and cold beer and was memorialized in the song "Luckenbach, Texas," by Waylon Jennings and Willie Nelson. Take a spin through the dance hall, buy a Shiner at the bar, and sit outside to watch up-and-coming or sometimes famous musicians pluck away at their guitars. After all, as the slogan says, "Everybody's somebody in Luckenbach." Open 9 a.m. daily with live music seven days a week.

LODGING For a quaint escape, you can't beat the **Hoffman Haus** (608 E. Creek St. in Fredericksburg; 830-997-6739; www.hoffmanhaus.com), a charming, rustic bed-and-breakfast located a block from Main Street. Features include a grand Great Hall perfect for relaxing with a book or hosting an event with friends; comfortable rooms that may include antique furnishings, private porches, and limestone fireplaces; and a day spa offering body and skin treatments and massages.

DAY 2/MORNING

BREAKFAST Start your day at the **Hoffman Haus** (608 E. Creek St. in Fredericksburg; 830-997-6739; www.hoffmanhaus.com), where breakfast is delivered to you in a basket each morning and a fresh selection of organic coffees and teas is available in your room.

Want to get out for breakfast? Head to Main Street and try **Rather Sweet Bakery and Café** (249 E. Main St.; 830-990-0498; www.rathersweet.com), which bakes up a host of fresh scones, tarts, cakes, brownies, and kolaches daily, as well as offers omelets, pancakes, breakfast tacos, oatmeal, and more. Don't miss the fantastic bacon cheddar scones. The cafe is also open for lunch. Open Mon through Sat at 8 a.m. Closed Sun.

Next, it's time to get some fresh air, so go northwest on US 290 east. Take Main Street to N. Llano Street/TX 16, then turn right on N. Milam Street/RR 965. Follow that to **Enchanted Rock State**

Natural Area (16710 Ranch Rd. 965 in Fredericksburg; 830-685-3636; www.tpwd.state.tx.us), one of the most beautiful areas in Texas. The highlight, of course, is the giant pink granite dome, which is hikeable for most skill levels and affords unrivaled views of the Hill Country. Other popular activities include camping, primitive backpacking, rock climbing, geological study, star gazing, bird-watching, and more. Day-use fees are $6 for those 13 and up.

Now, go south on RR 965 to US 290 and go left. Then, go right at RR 1376 until you hit Sisterdale Road and **SisterCreek Ranch** (1818 FM 1376 in Boerne; 830-324-6525; www.sistercreekranch .com) for an hour or two of horseback riding. The ranch, which features three creeks and lots of winding nature paths, also offers swimming, wildlife viewing, a spa, a saloon, and guesthouses for overnight stays. Call ahead for reservations and rates.

LUNCH Take RM 1376 north to 290 and go left. Follow that to US 87 north and go right until you see **Hill Top Café** (10661 N. Hwy 87; 830-997-8922; www.hilltopcafe.com). Featuring lunch and dinner daily, this laid-back joint prides itself on its full bar, live music, and great Southern specialties with both a Greek and Cajun flare. The restaurant is owned by Grammy award—winner Johnny Nicholas, so you know it's going to be fun.

Want live music closer to town? Hit up **Hondo's** (312 W. Main St.; 830-997-1633; www.hondosonmain.com), which features "gourmet Texas cuisine" such as donut burgers (the beef is actually formed in the shape of a doughnut), a fish taco salad, and hot gooey green shrimp dip. If you like spice, don't miss the Lip Burnin' Burger, which is mixed with spicy chipotle chiles and green onions and topped with roasted green chiles.

AFTERNOON

Now, it's time to get a taste of history. Take US 290 back to downtown Fredericksburg and stop at the **National Museum of the Pacific**

War (340 E. Main St.; 830-997-4379; www.nimitz-museum.org), which is dedicated to furthering the legacies of the more than 100,000 people who gave their lives as part of the Pacific and Asiatic Theaters in World War II. The museum features a George H. W. Bush Gallery, a memorial courtyard, a Japanese garden, and monuments to each of the presidents who served in WWII. Open daily from 9 a.m. to 5 p.m. Call for admission costs.

While you're on Main Street, stop in at **D'Vine Wine** (318 E. Main St.; 830-990-8466; http://fredericksburg.dvinewineusa .com), where you design your own labels to put on their bottles of wine. The winery and boutique also offers wine tasting at the tasting bar, where a flight of samples will cost you $5. Open Mon through Sat from 11 a.m. to 6 p.m. and Sun from 11 a.m. to 5 p.m.

Then, go 1 block over to E. San Antonio St. and stop at the **Pioneer Museum Complex** (312 W. San Antonio St.; 830-997-2835; http://pioneermuseum.net), a collection of structures from the 1800s that tells the story of life as it was for early settlers. The complex includes houses, a school, a bathhouse, and a former town hall. Open Mon through Sat from 10 a.m. to 5 p.m. and Sun from noon to 4 p.m. Admission is $5 for adults, $3 for ages 6–17, and free for children 5 and under.

DINNER Ready for a bite to eat? Stay on E. San Antonio and stop in at **August E's** (203 E. San Antonio; 830-997-1585; www.august-es.com), an upscale, artistic bistro serving "nouveau Texas cuisine" with menu items such as citrus truffle salad, signature crab stack, New Zealand lamb, mascarpone potatoes, and mesquite-grilled steaks. Don't miss the special Thai menu, when the restaurant dishes up Thai favorites. Call ahead for dates and times. Open daily for lunch and dinner. Reservations are recommended.

Want something a little more rustic? Try the fine **Navajo Grill** (803 E. Main St.; 830-990-8289; www.navajogrill.com), which features a covered patio bar and a gourmet menu filled with Southern favorites such as cedar planked salmon filets, bone-in pork chops, and green chile white cheddar corn grits. Open daily at 5:30 p.m. Reservations recommended.

DAY 3/MORNING

BREAKFAST   No trip to Fredericksburg would be complete without some classic German pastries, so before you head home, start your day at the **Old German Bakery** (225 W. Main St.; 830-997-9084), where sweet treats such as danishes, kolaches, and cream puffs are the order of the day. Grab some to go, or have a seat in the full restaurant, which features German-style breakfast and lunch items.

There's More . . . .

Drive. **Willow City Loop.** A scenic, 13-mile drive that offers gorgeous views of the Hill Country. Starts at SR 16 and continues to RR 1323; www.fredericksburgtexas-online.com/ftowillowcityloop.html.

History. **Fort Martin Scott Historical Site.** Restored U.S. Army outpost, 1606 E. Main St.; (830) 997-9895.

Gish's Old West Museum. Huge collection of Old West artifacts. Call ahead for an appointment. 502 N. Milam; (830) 997-2794.

Horse-drawn Carriage Tours. Guided carriage rides through the Historic District. Call for details at (830) 685-3454 or (830) 992-0700.

Nature. **Wildseed Farm.** Wildflower farm, nursery, and seed market at 100 Legacy Dr. in Fredericksburg; (800) 848-0078; www.wild seedfarms.com.

Wildlife. **Bats of Old Tunnel Wildlife Management Area.** A bat population that emerges nightly to search for food can be found at

10619 Old San Antonio Rd. in Fredericksburg; (866) 978-2287; www.tpwd.state.tx.us.

Special Events & Festivals . . . .

APRIL

Hill Country Run Motorcycle Rally, Luckenbach. An annual rally held in Luckenbach that benefits the Optimist Club; www.hillcountryrun .com.

San Angelo Wine & Food Festival, San Angelo. Weekend of wine and food tasting hosted by the San Angelo Cultural Affairs Council; (325) 653-6793; www.sanangeloarts.com.

MAY

Fredericksburg Crawfish Festival, Fredericksburg. A celebration of mudbugs that includes music, dancing, and, of course, plenty of crawfish. Held in the downtown Marktplatz; www.tex-fest.com /crawfish.

JULY

Gourmet Chile Pepper & Salsa Festival, Fredericksburg. Featuring gourmet food, hot air balloons, live entertainment, and more. Held at Wildseed Farm, 100 Legacy Dr. in Fredericksburg; (800) 848-0078; www.tex-fest.com/gcp.

Night in Old Fredericksburg, Fredericksburg. A chance to celebrate Fredericksburg as it used to be, with German dancing, folk music, food, and more; www.tex-fest.com/niof.

OCTOBER

Fredericksburg Food & Wine Fest, Fredericksburg. Appreciation of wine and food with music, craft booths, a food court, and more. Held in the downtown Marktplatz; www.fbgfoodandwinefest.com.

Oktoberfest, Fredericksburg. A full German celebration of beer, food, and music. Held in the downtown Marktplatz; (830) 997-4810; www.oktoberfestinfbg.com.

Other Recommended Restaurants & Lodgings . . . . .

FREDERICKSBURG
Altdorf Biergarten, 301 W. Main St.; (830) 997-7865; www .altdorfbiergarten-fbg.com. Outdoor biergarten with a wide menu including burgers, Tex-Mex, and salads.

Der Lindenbaum, 312 E. Main St.; (830) 997-9126; www.derlin denbaum.com. Fine German restaurant with steaks, sandwiches, and desserts.

Fredericksburg Brewing Co., 245 E. Main St.; (830) 997-1646; www.yourbrewery.com. Fun brewing company with a biergarten and restaurant.

Inn on Barons Creek, 308 S. Washington St.; (866) 990-0202; www.innonbaronscreek.com. Lovely hotel close to everything.

Magnolia House, 101 E. Hackberry St.; (830) 997-0306; www .magnolia-house.com. Gorgeous B&B with a fabulous breakfast.

Pasta Bella, 103 S. Llano St.; (830) 990-9778. Delicious Italian food.

Town Creek B&B, 706 W. Main St.; (830) 997-8396; www.cottages atlimestone.com. B&B for all types of travelers.

Two Wee Cottages Bed & Breakfast, 108 E. Morse St.; (877) 437-7739; www.2weecottages.com. Relaxing, quaint B&B in the center of it all.

For More Information . . . .

City of Fredericksburg; www.fbgtx.org.

Fredericksburg Chamber of Commerce; www.fredericksburg-texas .com.

Hill Country travel information; www.hill-country-visitor.com.

WESTBOUND ESCAPE *Four*

Hill Country Two— Gruene and New Braunfels

SUN, SUDS, AND SOUNDS IN THE LUSH HILL COUNTRY / 1 NIGHT

Laid-back vibe

Water activities

Country charm

Shopping

Dancing

When you visit a place where the motto is, "Gently resisting change since 1872," you can expect a certain laid-back, stick-to-your roots attitude. But don't think that makes this tiny music- and food-loving town—located halfway between Austin and San Antonio—sleepy. In fact, a visit to Gruene is quite the opposite: a water-splashing, foot-stomping riot in the tradition of the early settlers, who knew how to have a good time.

Founded in the mid-1800s by German immigrants, the town initially centered around Henry D. Gruene's cotton farm, cotton gin, and dance hall. Today, Gruene Hall remains the pulse of the little town, welcoming local and national acts such as Jerry Jeff Walker, Willie Nelson, and Aaron Neville to its 1,000-capacity space.

DAY 1/MORNING

From Houston, take I-10 west about 160 miles until you see TX 46 (exit 607) to New Braunfels and go right. Take that about 10 miles and you'll hit Gruene.

BREAKFAST You can't beat Texas barbecue, and the town of Luling, which you'll pass on the way to Gruene, is home to one of the best joints in the state: **Luling Bar-B-Q** (709 E. Davis St.; 830-875-3848). Open at 7:30 a.m., this redbrick

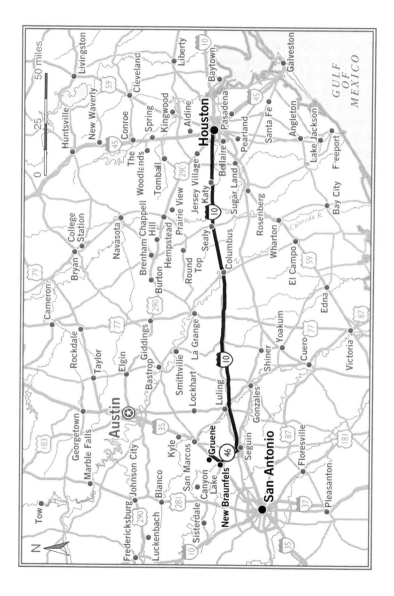

institution serves up combo plates with all the fixins, including slaw, potato salad, and mac and cheese. Cash, check, and credit cards accepted.

After breakfast, hop back on I-10 and follow signs to Seguin, a small town that's home to the **World's Second Largest Pecan** (on the north lawn of Guadalupe County Court House at the intersection of Highways 123 and 90A). That's right—second largest. Brunswick, Missouri, stole the title from Seguin several years ago, but in Seguin that doesn't matter: The town still proudly calls itself the "pecan capital of the world," and it's worth a stop to get a photo next to the giant concrete nut.

Once you get on TX 46, take it to Gruene Road, where you'll see the entrance to **Rockin' R River Rides** (1405 Gruene Rd. in New Braunfels; 800-553-5628; www.rockinr.com). Tubing (or "toobing," as the locals say) is a quintessential Texas activity from spring to fall. Just park, ice down your cooler, pick up your toobs, and hit the water on the Guadalupe or Comal River. As you float, enjoy the refreshing emerald water and the willow and cypress trees that line the banks. Rockin' R provides transportation back to the parking lot at the end of the river ride, so the only thing you need to worry about is not getting burned to a crisp by the end of the afternoon.

LUNCH Instantly recognizable by its position just under Gruene's symbolic water tower, the **Gristmill River Restaurant and Bar** (1287 Gruene Rd.; 830-625-0684; www.gristmillrestaurant.com) is a local favorite known for its delicious chicken-fried steak; famous clientele such as George Strait, John Travolta, and Mary Lou Retton; and gorgeous outside deck overlooking the Guadalupe River. You're going to want a hearty lunch after a day on the river, and the Gristmill is the perfect place to get it. Built in the location of a former water-powered mill, the Gristmill was placed on the National Register of Historic Places in 1975 and today serves thousands of people who visit craving down-home food in a relaxing setting.

AFTERNOON

After lunch, take some time to wander the town's charming shops. Start at the **Gruene General Store** (1610 Hunter Rd. in New Braunfels; 800-974-8353; www.gruenegeneralstore.com), the only business to continue operating after a boll weevil epidemic nearly destroyed the town in the 1920s. The store claims to have something for everyone, and between its selection of vintage signs, jalapeño jellies, homemade fudge, cookbooks, antiques, and soda fountain, I'd say that's accurate. Don't miss the 5-cent coffee.

Next, cross the street to **Gruene Antique Company** (1607 Hunter Rd.; 830-629-7781; www.grueneantiqueco.com), which has been offering antiques, collectibles, and gifts to visitors since 1986. The building, which is considered a Texas landmark, once housed the town's post office and is still home to the original bank vault.

Want something a little more current? Check out the **Dancing Bear** (1632 Hunter Rd.; 830-629-2059; www.dancingbeartexas .com), an adorable gift shop in a Victorian-style house thoughtfully divided by theme, such as a "kitchen room," "children's room," "Western room," and "garden room." And don't forget to take a look out back during your visit. The shop's sprawling "Gruene Gardens" have everything for your inner gardener, including stakes, feeders, stepping-stones, wind chimes, and handcrafted pottery.

Take your time browsing the many other stores in the square, then wander down to **The Grapevine** (1612 Hunter Rd.; 830-606-0093; www.grapevineingruene.com), a fun, comfortable wine tasting room featuring more than one hundred local wines, as well as beer, gourmet food, and wine accessories and decor. This is a great spot to enjoy a glass while soaking up the city's carefree mentality on the wide front porch. Free tastings are offered daily, and wine is sold by the glass or bottle. Open daily at 10 a.m.

DINNER Getting hungry after all of that shopping? Take Hunter Road to Gruene Road and go left to the **Gruene River Grill** (1259 Gruene Rd.; 830-624-2300; www.gruenerivergrill.com), a rustic, Texas-centric spot where you'll feel comfortable in anything from flip-flops to high heels. The atmosphere at this spot, which overlooks the Guadalupe River, can't be beat, and neither can the food, with signature items such as crispy shrimp wontons, jalapeño-glazed shrimp brochettes, Southwestern meat loaf, balsamic rib eye, and pan-seared redfish. The restaurant also offers a full bar—I recommend the frozen peach bellini.

NIGHTLIFE Wrap up your day in Gruene with a show at the historic **Gruene Hall** (1281 Gruene Rd.; 830-606-1281; www.gruenehall.com), a Texas legend—and the oldest dance hall in Texas—where the wood planks are worn, the Shiner beers are cold, and the people couldn't be friendlier. Built in 1878, this 6,000-square-foot building still looks like it would have in the early days, with features such as a tin roof and side flaps for an open-air feel. In the beginning, the hall hosted not just weekly dances but other events as well, such as high school graduations and even badger fights. Today, whether you catch a legend such as Kenny Wayne Shepherd, Bob Schneider, or Joe Ely on the inside stage or simply enjoy a game of washers in the backyard, this place will take you far away from your troubles. Live music is offered seven nights a week, as well as Sat and Sun afternoons. Fri and Sat night shows typically require a cover charge—otherwise admission is free. Kids are welcome for all nonticketed shows. A gospel brunch is also offered on the second Sun of each month.

LODGING Want a place that's convenient to all the local attractions but also offers a sweet respite within its walls? **Gruene River Inn** (1111 Gruene Rd.; 830-627-1600; www.grueneriverinn.com) is just the spot. Rooms include balconies that overlook the river, as well as whirlpool tubs and fireplaces. Rates start around $150.

DAY 2/MORNING

BREAKFAST Enjoy a breakfast buffet including fresh breakfast tacos, juices, muffins, waffles, cereal, and coffee at **Gruene River Inn,** included with your stay.

Next, head south on Gruene Road and go right on Common Street, then right on N. Liberty Avenue. Take Liberty Avenue to W. Austin Street and go left until you see signs for **Schlitterbahn Waterpark** (305 W. Austin St.; 830-625-2351; www.schlitterbahn.com). This is one of the oldest and best water parks in the country, so you're going to want to plan to spend at least a morning.

The park is divided into three sections. I recommend starting at **Blastenhoff**—home to attractions such as the Black Knight Tunnel Slides (think tubing in total darkness), the Master Blaster uphill water coaster, the family-friendly Wolfpack raft slide, and the wave-ridden Torrent River.

Next, hit the rides at **Schlitterbahn West,** the original park which is still home to some of its best rides, including the Soda Straw body slides and the Whitewater, Cliffhanger, Hillside, and Raging River tube chutes.

Finally, wrap up your day at **Surfenburg,** where you can try your hand at boogie boarding, soak in the Dragon's Lair hot tub, or chill with the kids at the Squirt 'n Sliden Kiddie Park.

The park is typically open May through Sept. Tickets are around $40 for an adult day pass and $30 for children and seniors. Coolers and picnic lunches are allowed, and concessions are available.

LUNCH After all of that activity, you're going to be ready to fuel up, so head back to Gruene for lunch at **Adobe Verde** (1724 Hunter Rd.; 830-629-0777; www.adobeverde.com). Featuring great nachos, margaritas, and a playground for the kids, you're sure to keep everyone entertained and well fed. Happy hour is Mon through Fri from 3 to 6:30 p.m. Live music Thurs through Sun.

AFTERNOON

By now you're bound to need a break from the sun, so take TX 46 west to FM 1863, go left and take that until you hit **Natural Bridge Caverns** (26495 Natural Bridge Caverns Rd. in San Antonio; 210-651-6101; www.naturalbridgecaverns.com), which has an average year-round temperature of 70 degrees. At the caverns, which are home to some incredible formations, towers, pools, and bridges, you can go caving, rock climbing, or even pan for precious stones. Wear walking shoes, as some areas are slippery when wet. Open year-round; various packages are available.

Once you're finished spelunking, go southeast on FM 3009 until you hit I-35 south and take that to the very strange yet entertaining **Animal World and Snake Farm** (5640 I-35 south in New Braunfels; 830-608-9270; www.exoticanimalworld.com). If you drive this corridor often, you've no doubt seen the signs for this place, which houses 500 types of snakes and animals such as zebras, lemurs, crocodiles, and monkeys. To walk in to is be immediately overwhelmed—when I was there a giant boa constrictor was wrapped around a group of kids posing for pictures—but also awed by the pure mystique (and in some cases beauty) of these creatures. Plus, at $9.75 for adults, $6.75 for children 3–12, and free for kids 2 and under, it's cheaper than visiting the zoo. Open daily year-round from 10 a.m. to 6 p.m.

DINNER   Before you hit the road for home, follow signs from the highway to the I-35 Business Route north and take that until you reach the **New Braunfels Smokehouse** (1090 North Business I-35; 830-625-2416; www.nbsmokehouse.com), where favorites include the chopped brisket sandwich, the turkey and bacon salad sandwich, the "world-famous" stuffed tomato, and chicken and dumplings. And be sure to take a few slices of their scrumptious homemade pies with you, even if chances are good they won't make it past the ride home.

There's More . . . .

Kids. **McKenna Children's Museum.** Multifaceted, interactive space for children of all ages. 801 W. San Antonio St.; (830) 606-9525; www.mckennakids.org.

Museum. **New Braunfels Museum of Art and Music.** Tribute to Texas's cultural contributions in art and music. 1259 Gruene Rd.; (830) 625-5636.

Outdoors. **Gruene Outfitters.** Fly-fishing lessons and gear. 1629 Hunter Rd.; (830) 625-4440; www.grueneoutfitters.com.

Park. **Guadalupe River State Park.** This riverfront park offers outdoor activities such as canoeing, swimming, fishing, tubing, picnicking, hiking, and camping. 3350 Park Road 31 in Spring Branch; (830) 438-2656; www.tpwd.state.tx.us.

Sports. **Texas Ski Ranch.** Seventy-acre multisport facility offering wakeboarding, skateboarding, motocross, and rock climbing. 6700 I-35 north in New Braunfels; (830) 627-2843; www.texasskiranch .com.

Special Events & Festivals . . . .

YEAR-ROUND
Gruene Market Days, Gruene. More than one hundred vendors converge with arts and crafts on the third weekend of every month, Feb to Nov, and the first weekend of Dec. (830) 832-1721; www .gruenemarketdays.com.

MAY
Americana Music Jam, Gruene. A tribute to Americana music at Gruene Hall that benefits children's charities. (830) 629-5077; www.gruenehall.com.

SEPTEMBER
Texas Metal Arts Festival, Gruene. The best metal artists (think sculpture, not Slayer) in Texas converge. (903) 852-3311; www .texasmetalarts.com.

OCTOBER
Gruene Music and Wine Fest, Gruene. Wine- and music-centric festival benefitting the United Way of Comal County. (830) 629-5077; www.gruenemusicandwinefest.org.

Texas Clay Festival, Gruene. Demos, classes, hands-on activities, and items for sale made by Texas's best potters. (830) 629-7975; www.texasclayfestival.com.

Tour de Gruene, Gruene. Bicycle tour with multiple route lengths benefitting local charities. (210) 862-3524; www.tourdegruene.com.

Wurstfest, New Braunfels. Ten-day celebration of all things German, including the absolute best wurst. 178 Landa Park Dr.; (830) 625-9167; www.wurstfest.com.

Other Recommended Restaurants & Lodgings . . . . .

GRUENE
Gruene Apple B&B, 1235 Gruene Rd.; (830) 643-1234; www.gruene apple.com. Gourmet bed-and-breakfast on the Guadalupe River.

Gruene Mansion Inn, 1275 Gruene Rd.; (830) 629-2641; www .gruenemansioninn.com. Upscale, perfectly decorated B&B.

Gruene Onion Grill, 1324 Common St.; (830) 629-2989; www .grueneoniongrill.com. Classic, upscale fare with a martini room next door.

NEW BRAUNFELS
The Faust Hotel, 240 S. Seguin Ave.; (830) 625 7791; www.faust hotel.com. Small, charming hotel in New Braunfels.

Holiday Inn Hotel New Braunfels, 1051 I-35 east; (830) 625-8017; www.holidayinn.com.

Mozie's Bar and Grill, 1601 Hunter Rd.; (830) 515-1281; www .moziesbarandgrill.com. Bar and grill with a solid menu and TVs for watching the game.

Pat's Place, 202 S. Union Ave.; (830) 625-9070. Casual spot popular with the post-Schlitterbahn crowd.

For More Information . . . .

General New Braunfels information; www.newbraunfels-tx.net.

Gruene Tourism Board, 1601 Hunter Rd.; (830) 629-5077; www .gruenetexas.com.

New Braunfels Chamber of Commerce, 390 South Seguin Ave.; (800) 572-2626; www.nbcham.org.

WESTBOUND ESCAPE *Five*
Hill Country Three— Lockhart and San Marcos
DEEP IN THE HEART OF TEXAS BARBECUE / 2 NIGHTS

Delicious barbecue
Water activities
Historical attractions
Shiner brewery
Extreme sports

Nothing is more beloved in Texas than barbecue. So when you travel to the barbecue capital of the state, you can expect a town that takes its smokin'—and eating—seriously. That's what it's like to visit Lockhart, a small town of about 12,000 that is home to four of the best barbecue joints in the world. While you're at it, hit up the tiny town of Shiner, home to Texas's favorite homegrown beer, for a tour of the brewery.

In nearby San Marcos, base of Texas State University, the fun continues with outdoor activities, nightlife, shopping, historical attractions, and great food. From skydiving to Shiner sipping, you can expect a visit to this area to fill your weekend, and your belly, with a time to remember.

DAY 1/MORNING

From Houston, take I-10 west to US 183 (which turns into TX 80 as you reach San Marcos).

BREAKFAST Just before you reach the US 183 exit, exit in Columbus and go right on TX 71 BR, then right on Milam Street to **Schobel's Restaurant** (2020 Milam St.; 979-732-2385; www.schobelsrestaurant.com). A local favorite and regular pit stop for Houstonians headed to Austin, the restaurant opens at 6 a.m. daily

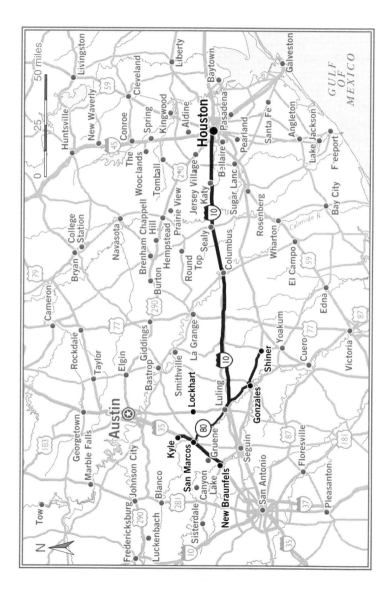

and serves breakfast until 11 a.m. Menu offerings include ham and eggs, omelets, pancakes, waffles, breakfast burritos, and a variety of eggs Benedict. Don't miss The Hudson, which is made with fried eggs, homemade sausage, buttermilk biscuits, cheddar cheese, and sausage gravy served with hash browns and grits.

Next, go north on Milam and left on Washington Street to the **Mary Elizabeth Hopkins Santa Claus Museum** (604 Washington St.; 979-732-5135), home to more than 2,000 Santas. Hopkins started her collection in 1913 and had a wide variety when she died in 1990. Items on display include Santa-themed art by Norman Rockwell, Coca-Cola Santas, and life-size Santas. Call ahead to make an appointment.

Got your fill of Christmas spirit? Take Milam Street back to I-10 west and go right. Take that until you reach TX 97 and go left, then take a left on Smith Street to reach the **Gonzales Memorial Museum** (414 Smith St.; 830-672-6350; www.cityofgonzales .org). The most exciting artifact here is the Come and Take It cannon, which may have fired the first shot for Texas independence in 1835. The museum itself is also a work of art, featuring a grand rotunda, amphitheater, and marble memorial mural.

After that, go north on Spur 146 to US Alt. 90 and go east for 8 miles. Then, go left on CR 361 until you see the entrance for the McClure-Braches House on the left and the **Sam Houston Oak** (www .gonzalestexas.com), the tall, sprawling oak where Sam Houston was said to have learned about the fall of the Alamo and sent orders to General Fannin to retreat from Goliad. At sunrise on March 14, 1836, Houston got on his horse at that site and left with 374 men riding east toward San Jacinto, where they would eventually meet Santa Anna in the Battle of San Jacinto.

Want some more history? Trek back over to US Alt. 90 and go southeast until you hit the city of Shiner and the **Spoetzl Brewery** (603 E. John Hybner Way in Shiner; 361-594-3383; www.shiner

.com). The oldest independent brewery in Texas (it was founded in 1909), Spoetzl pumps out 635 bottles a minute and 15,000 cases of beer each day. All of the beers brewed at Spoetzl take at least thirty days to create. The brewery tour includes a visit to the brew house, fermentation tanks, bottling room, keg line, warehouse, and hospitality room. Free tours are offered weekdays at 11 a.m. and 1:30 p.m. The gift shop is open from 9 a.m. to 5 p.m. weekdays and 11 a.m. to 3 p.m. Sat, with an hour lunch break at 1:30.

LUNCH Nothing goes better with beer than barbecue, so make your way to **Lockhart,** the barbecue capital of Texas.

Go west on US Alt. 90 until you reach N. Joseph Street/US 183 BR and go right on US 183 north. Once you reach Lockhart, go right on N. Magnolia Avenue/US 183 until you reach N. Colorado Street and see **Kreuz Market** (619 N. Colorado St.; 512-398-2361; www.kreuzmarket.com), considered by many to be the best of the best. Home to a huge list of meats and a bright, friendly atmosphere, this is real-deal Texas barbecue. But don't get too full—there are three other must-try barbecue joints in Lockhart as well. Once you've sampled Kreuz, go south on US 183 to Market Street and go right, then turn left on S. Commerce Street and stop at **Smitty's Market** (208 S. Commerce; 512-398-9344; www.smittysmarket.com). The menu here is smaller than the one at Kreuz, but the flavor is just as big. In fact, the two barbecue joints are run by siblings who disagreed about how the business should be run after inheriting it from their father. One took the name and opened a brand-new facility (Kreuz), while the other kept the original location and renamed it in memory of their father (Smitty's). The two other joints not to be missed are **Black's Barbecue** (215 N. Main St.; 888-632-8225; www.blacksbbq.com) and **Chisholm Trail Bar-B-Q** (1323 S. Colorado St.; 512-398-6027).

AFTERNOON

Work off that lunch by taking S. Colorado Street to E. Market Street and going right. Then, take a right on State Park Road until you reach

Lockhart State Park and Golf Course (2012 State Park Rd.; 512-398-3479; www.tpwd.state.tx.us). This 264-acre park offers picnicking, camping, fishing, hiking, nature study, and a nine-hole golf course operated by the state park system. Weekday greens fees are $9; weekend/holiday greens fees are $11. A recreation hall with a patio, picnic area, playground equipment, and a kitchen is available for day use, as is a swimming pool. Interesting fact: In 1840, the Battle of Plum Creek was fought just a few miles from the park to the north.

Next, head back to E. Market Street to the **Caldwell County Museum** (315 E. Market St.; www.lockhart-tx.org), which was built in 1908 and once served as the Caldwell County Jail. The redbrick, five-story building contains nine cells, a basement for storage and a ground floor where the sheriff lived. The museum is operated by the Caldwell County Historical Commission and is open on weekends from 1 to 5 p.m.

Finally, go west on E. Market Street to S. Commerce Street and go right to TX 142/E. San Antonio Street. Go left, then take a right on TX 80/San Marcos Hwy. When you reach I-35, go left to the **Power Olympic Outdoor Center** (602 I-35 north; 512-203-0093; www.kayakinstruction.org). The center offers a variety of whitewater and flatwater kayaking and canoeing classes aimed at all skill levels. Located on the San Marcos River's Rio Vista Falls, this scenic location is perfect for paddling.

DINNER Getting hungry? Go northeast on I-35 north to River Road and take a left on RR 12/TX 80 and follow that to Moore Street until you reach **Palmer's Restaurant** (218 Moore St.; 512-353-3500; www.palmerstexas.com). Located in a renovated home from the 1920s, this restaurant offers large portions, fresh cocktails, and a gorgeous courtyard. Menu items include a "French country dinner" with a salad, soup, and house wine, as well as baked fondue with spinach and artichoke hearts and pecan-crusted salmon. Grab a spot by the fountain, order a Damiana margarita, and enjoy the breeze. Open daily at 11 a.m.

Want something a little more up-tempo? Visit **San Marcos River Pub and Grill** (701 Cheatham St.; 512-353-3747; www.riverpubandgrill.com), with a full menu of sandwiches, salads, and appetizers. The restaurant also offers a riverfront patio bar that's perfect for a cold drink.

NIGHTLIFE After dinner, check out **Cheatham Street Warehouse** (119 Cheatham St.; 512-353-3777; www.cheathamstreet.com), a live music venue that's a hub for up-and-coming Texas artists such as Wade Bowen and Randy Rogers. Or check out **Riley's Tavern** (8894 FM 1102 in New Braunfels; 512-392-3132; www .rileystavern.com), which calls itself "Texas's first tavern after Prohibition." Open daily Sun through Fri from 1 p.m. to midnight and Sat from 1 p.m. to 1 a.m.

LODGING After your long day of sightseeing, lay your head at the **Crystal River Inn** (324 W. Hopkins in San Marcos; 888-396-3739). This 1883-era Victorian inn offers everything from themed getaways, gourmet breakfasts, horse-drawn carriage rides, canopy beds, and sprawling oak trees. The thirteen on-site rooms vary and may include private baths, fireplaces, four-poster beds, covered porches, and more. Because the inn is located in the heart of downtown, it is convenient to most everything.

DAY 2/MORNING

BREAKFAST Start your day with a delicious breakfast at **Crystal River Inn** (324 W. Hopkins in San Marcos; 888-396-3739), which features dishes such as eggs Benedict, bananas Foster crepes, raspberry French toast at brunch, or homemade muffins in the rose garden.

All fueled up? Good, because you're going to need that energy for your next event. Go east on RR 12/W. Hopkins Street (Hopkins Street becomes TX 80). Go right on FM 20, then left on Barber Street/CR 273 until you reach **Skydive San Marcos** (517 Airfield

Rd. in Fentress; 512-488-2214; www.skydivesanmarcos.com), a skydiving facility near San Marcos where beginners may make a tandem skydive from over 10,000 feet over the Hill Country with an experienced instructor. Call ahead to make a reservation.

Once your heart rate has settled, go northwest on Barber Street/CR 273 to FM 20 and go right. Then, go left on TX 80, right on Charles Austin Drive, and right on Aquarena Springs Drive/US 81/TX 82 to **Aquarena Nature Center** (601 University Dr.; 512-245-7570; www.aquarena.txstate.edu). Texas State University's Aquarena Nature Center is home to a Diving for Science program that involves diving in San Marcos Springs, an aquarium, a wetlands boardwalk, and the famous glass-bottom boat tours of the San Marcos River. Tours are thirty minutes and cost $8 for adults, $7 for seniors, and $6 for children 4–15 and are free for children under 4.

Next, go southwest on Aquarena Springs Drive/TX 82 toward Charles Austin Drive. Follow TX 82 until it becomes N. CM Allen Parkway, then turn right on RR 12/E. Hopkins Street. Next, turn right on N. Johnson Avenue, left on Belvin Street, right on Quarry Street, and right on Prospect Street to **Wonder World Park** (1000 Prospect St.; 512-392-6711; www.wonderworldpark.com). Home to an earthquake-formed cave, a wildlife petting park, a 190-foot observation tower, and an antigravity house, this place will keep your whole clan entertained for hours. Open daily. Call for hours and ticket prices.

LUNCH Go southwest on Prospect Street, left on N. Bishop Street, then right on W. Hopkins to Wonder World Drive until it hits I-35 and go north. Take exit 213 to FM 150/Kyle, then go left on E. Center Street/RR 150/FM 150, then go right on N. Old Highway 81 to **Milt's Pit BBQ** (905 North Old TX 81; 512-268-4734). This great little place offers delicious barbecue in a casual atmosphere. Don't miss Milt's Haystack, a melt-in-your-mouth "bird's nest"–style sandwich.

Just in it for dessert? Try **Texas Pie Co.** (202 W. Center St.; 512-268-5885; www.texaspiecompany.com), where the comfort food isn't bad and the pies are even better, ranging from peach and Dutch apple to chocolate fudge and peanut butter mousse.

AFTERNOON

Spend the afternoon wandering the historic streets of Kyle, starting with the **Katherine Anne Porter Literary Center** (508 W. Center St.; 512-268-6637; www.english.txstate.edu/kap), the childhood home of author and Pulitzer Prize winner Katherine Anne Porter. Tours of the home are available by appointment.

Next, visit the **Claiborne Kyle Log House** (2400 S. Old Stagecoach Rd. off CR 136; www.kylechamber.org/KylesRecreation Attractions.php), which was built in 1850 out of cedar logs by slave labor for Claiborne Kyle, a Mississippi senator who later became a member of the Texas Legislature. The house is in the National Register of Historic Places and has been the site of a Texas Historical Marker since 1982.

DINNER Wrap up your day with dinner at **Bordeaux's** (108 Center St., 512-268-3463; www.bordeauxs.net), a steak and seafood house with an impressive martini bar. Menu items include deep-fried mozzarella medallions, escargot, broiled Australian lobster tail, pepper-crusted New York strip, and more. Open Tues through Thurs from 5:30 to 9 p.m. and Fri and Sat from 5:30 to 10 p.m. Reservations are recommended.

DAY 3/MORNING

BREAKFAST Again, start your day with a delicious breakfast at **Crystal River Inn** (324 W. Hopkins in San Marcos; 888-396-3739), which features dishes such as eggs Benedict, bananas Foster crepes, raspberry French toast at brunch, or homemade muffins in the rose garden.

Then, head to I-35 and go north to the **Tanger Outlet Center** (4015 I-35 south; 512-396-7446; www.tangeroutlet.com/sanmarcos). This sprawling outlet mall has every type of shop you can imagine, including Calvin Klein, Kenneth Cole, Hot Topic, The Children's Place, Charlotte Russe, Coldwater Creek, Esprit, Luggage Factory, and Vans. Check online for special discounts and coupons.

After that, head next door to **Prime Outlets** (3939 I-35 south; 512-396-2200; www.primeoutlets.com), a mecca for every type of upscale shopping outlet store you desire. Stores include Barneys New York, BCBG Max Azria, Betsey Johnson, Coach, Crate & Barrel, Fendi, Gucci, Kate Spade, Nike, 7 for All Mankind, and more. Check the website for special discounts and coupons.

LUNCH Before you head home, grab lunch at the **Cracker Barrel Old Country Store** (4321 I-35 south; 512-353-4122; www.crackerbarrel.com), everyone's favorite down-home restaurant. Menu items include chicken-fried steak, chicken and dumplings, and fried chicken. The best part? Once you're done with dinner, you can head next door to the adjacent store to buy kitschy souvenirs.

There's More . . . .

Kids. **Playscape at Children's Park.** Incredible 20,000-square-foot playscape with seventy play stations and a skateboard trail. 205 S. CM Allen Parkway in San Marcos.

Sports. **Lost Paintball.** Full-service paintball facility with multiple fields. Off Hilliard Road near I-35; (512) 757-0410; www.secfoot ball.net/paintball.

Sunset Bowling Lanes. Local bowling alley especially popular with students. 1304 Hwy 123; (512) 396-2334; www.sunsetbowling lanes.com.

Thunder Hill Raceway. Car racing near San Marcos. 24801 I-35 in Kyle; (512) 262-1352; www.thunderhillraceway.com.

Water. **San Marcos Lions Tube Rental.** Rents inner tubes so you can float the San Marcos River. City Park between University Drive and Ranch Road 12; (512) 396-5466; www.tubesanmarcos.com.

Special Events & Festivals . . . .

APRIL

Texas Hill Country Food and Wine Festival. A weekend of wine tasting and food sampling. Various Hill Country locations; (512) 249-6300; www.texaswineandfood.org.

JUNE

Texas State International Piano Festival, San Marcos. A weekend of recitals and master classes for pianists from around the country; www.music.txstate.edu/piano.

DECEMBER

San Marcos Christmas Festival, San Marcos. Lights, shopping, and holiday cheer in the heart of San Marcos; www.sights-n-sounds.org.

Other Recommended Restaurants & Lodgings . . . . .

KYLE

Inn Above Onion Creek, 4444 W. FM 150 in Kyle; (512) 268-1617; www.innaboveonioncreek.com. Beautiful bed-and-breakfast with quaint features.

Lucky Cup Coffee House, 108 Front St. in Kyle; (512) 535-5636. Coffee, pastries, and wraps in a cool atmosphere.

Luvianos, 804 W. Center St. in Kyle; (512) 268-4380. Dependable Tex-Mex with a full bar.

LOCKHART
Best Western Lockhart Hotel and Suites, 1811 S. Colorado St. in Lockhart; (512) 620-0300; www.bestwestern.com. Affordable lodging convenient to Lockhart attractions.

Lockhart Inn, 1207 S. Colorado St. in Lockhart; (512) 398-5201; www.lockhartinntexas.com. Newly remodeled, centrally located inn.

Plum Creek Inn, 2001 Hwy 183 south in Lockhart; (512) 398-4911; www.plumcreekinn.net. Motel with an on-site Tex-Mex restaurant.

SAN MARCOS
Café on the Square, 126 N. LBJ Dr.; (512) 396-9999. Nice, casual spot for breakfast, lunch, and dinner.

Cool Mint Café, 415 Burleson St.; (512) 396-2665; www.coolmintcafe.com. Delicious, contemporary American cuisine.

La Quinta San Marcos, 1619 I-35 north in San Marcos; (512) 392-8800; www.lq.com. Centered, convenient lodging.

Root Cellar Café, 215 North LBJ Dr. in San Marcos; (512) 392-5158; www.rootcellarcafe.com. Breakfast, lunch, dinner and drinks, with an art gallery on the side.

Sean Patrick's Irish Pub and Texas Grub, 202 E. San Antonio St., Ste. 119; (512) 392-7310; www.seanpatrickstx.com. Lunch, dinner, and drinks on the San Marcos square.

For More Information . . . .

City of Gonzales; www.cityofgonzales.org.

City of Kyle; www.cityofkyle.com.

City of Lockhart; www.lockhart-tx.org.

City of San Marcos; www.ci.san-marcos.tx.us/tourism.

Lockhart Chamber of Commerce; www.lockhartchamber.com.

San Marcos Convention and Visitor Bureau; www.toursanmarcos.com.

Texas Barbecue Trail; www.texasbbqtrail.com/lockhart.

WESTBOUND ESCAPE *Six*

San Antonio
ESCAPE TO ALAMO CITY / 2 NIGHTS

The Alamo

Historic missions

River Walk activities

Shopping

Theme parks

Of all the places to visit in Texas, this one is the most popular. Between its incredible history, its family-friendly River Walk, its extensive dining and shopping options, and its multicultural vibe, there really is a little something for everyone to do.

Once the largest Spanish settlement in Texas, San Antonio played a large role throughout the state's history, the most notable incident being the Battle of the Alamo.

Today, San Antonio is the second-largest city in Texas, with a population of approximately 1.3 million. With so many attractions, from major theme parks such as Six Flags Fiesta Texas and Sea-World to historic icons such as the Alamo and the San Antonio Missions National Historical Park, you can rest assured that everyone in your clan will have a fun-filled, educational visit.

DAY 1/MORNING

To get to San Antonio, simply take I-10 west for about 195 miles.

Make a pit stop at **Buc-ee's** (10070 I-10 west in Luling; 830-875-6811; www.bucees.com), a convenience store/gas station known for sparkling bathrooms, great snack and breakfast food, and its unmistakable logo: a grinning beaver wearing a bright red cap. When you stop, be sure to pick up a bag of Beaver Nuggets, a puffed, sugar-coated concoction perfect for consuming by the handful.

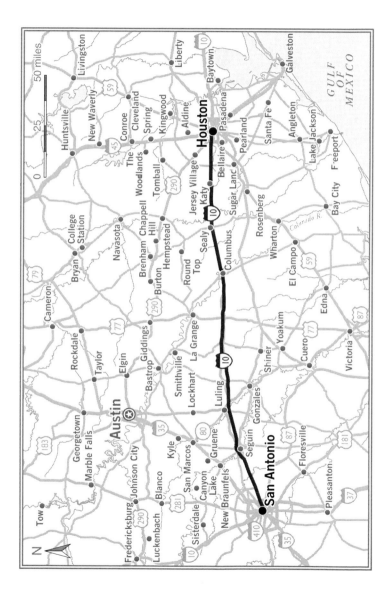

BREAKFAST Want something more substantial than Beaver Nuggets? Once you get close to San Antonio, merge onto I-410 north from I-10 west via exit 581. Then, merge onto I-35 south and take exit 158C to TX 368 Loop/N. Alamo Street/ Broadway. Turn right on Broadway, then left on E. Grayson and end at **Osteria Il Sogno** (200 E. Grayson, Suite 100; 210-223-3900; www.pearlbrewery.com), located inside the new Pearl Brewery complex. A casual Italian eatery, Il Sogno charms with huge windows where you can watch the staff making homemade pasta and a lush outdoor courtyard that will transport you to Tuscany or Rome. Breakfast offerings include fruit platters, coffee cake, paninis, eggs, and fresh bread baskets. Don't miss the coddled eggs with truffle oil. Open for breakfast Tues through Fri from 7:30 a.m. to 10 a.m. and Sat from 8:30 a.m. to 10 a.m. No breakfast offered on Sun; closed Mon.

After breakfast, take some time to discover the rest of the **Pearl Brewery complex** (200 E. Grayson; 210-227-0221; www.pearl brewery.com). Located in the former home of the Pearl Brewery on the banks of the San Antonio River, this twenty-two-acre, multiuse development was created as the culinary and cultural anchor of the city's new Museum Reach district. The complex also hosts a farmers' market on Sat from 9 a.m. to 1 p.m.

Start at Melissa Guerra's **Tienda de Cocina** (200 E. Grayson; 210-293-3983; www.melissaguerra.com), a cookware and import store that features everything from upscale stand-up mixers to embroidered hi-tops to fine coffees. Don't miss the spectacular Mexican folk art offerings, such as the vibrant Loteria jewelry.

Then, head next door to **The Twig** (200 E. Grayson; 210-826-6411; http://thetwig.indiebound.com), a cool little local bookshop known for its attention to homegrown artists, from its "Twiglets" book club to its weekly story time to its friendly staff, who go out of their way to get the book you're looking for into your hands.

Next, visit the **Aveda Institute** (250 E. Grayson; 210-222-0023; www.avedaisa.com), a full-service salon where you can get your hair cut by an aspiring stylist for as little as $16. Other services include manicures, pedicures, color, facials, and waxing. Not in the mood for a service? Check out the salon shop, which features a full range of Aveda products.

Once you're shopped out, go north to E. Josephine Street and go right, then turn left on Broadway. Follow that to Austin Highway, go right and then take a slight left onto N. New Braunfels Avenue and go until you see the **McNay Art Museum** (6000 N. New Braunfels; 210-824-5368; www.mcnayart.org). One of San Antonio's best museums, the McNay is home to nearly 20,000 works including European and American pieces by artists such as Paul Cézanne, Vincent van Gogh, Auguste Rodin, Henri Matisse, Pablo Picasso, Edward Hopper, and Georgia O'Keeffe. Open daily except Mon. Call for times and admission information.

LUNCH Once you're ready for lunch, go south on N. New Braunfels Avenue, go right on Austin Highway, then turn left on Broadway Street and stop at a great little burger joint called **Cheesy Jane's** (4200 Broadway St.; 210-826-0800; www.cheesyjanes.com). The menu here includes a bunch of types of burgers (including turkey and veggie burgers), sliders, Tater Tots, onion rings, salads, chicken fingers, shakes, and malts. Don't miss the fantastic "spicy splinters"—battered and fried onion and jalapeño slivers served with ranch dressing. Shake flavors include peanut butter and jelly, dreamsicle, blue raspberry, amaretto espresso, chocolate cherry, and mint chocolate chip Oreo, just to name a few. Call for hours.

AFTERNOON

Now that you're all stuffed, go southwest on Broadway Street to Tuleta Drive and go right until you reach N. St. Mary's Street and **Brackenridge Park.** San Antonio's favorite park, Brackenridge houses a variety of activities that are fun for the whole family.

Start at the **Japanese Tea Garden** (3853 N. St. Mary's Street; 210-207-3053; www.sanantonio.gov), a lovely botanical garden run by the city's parks and recreation department. The park features a garden, floral display, shaded pathways, stone bridges, koi ponds, a 60-foot waterfall, and a renovated Jingu house. Open daily from dawn to dusk; admission is free.

Next, go next door to the **San Antonio Zoo and Aquarium** (3903 N. St. Mary's St.; 210-734-7184; www.sazoo-aq.org), where 3,500 animals representing 600 animal species coexist on fifty-six acres. Visitor favorites include the agile black leopards, the laid-back Malayan tapir, and the regal painted stork. Go early in the summer, however, as the park gets very hot by the afternoon. Open daily. Call for hours and admission.

After the zoo, it's time to get a taste of San Antonio history. From N. St. Mary's Street, go southwest to US 281 south and follow that to I-10 west/US 87 north via exit 139. From there, take the exit to TX 536 Spur/Probandt Street (exit 573) and follow that to Steves Avenue. Turn right on Steves, then right on Mission Road, and end at **Mission Concepcion** (807 Mission Rd.; 210-534-1540; www.nps.gov), one of San Antonio's historical missions that is part of the **San Antonio Missions National Historical Park**. A stone church that was dedicated in 1755, Mission Concepcion is the oldest unrestored stone church in America, with original frescoes still visible in some of the rooms. As you look up at the building, you can't help marveling at how much it looks like it must have appeared in the eighteenth century. Open daily from 9 a.m. to 5 p.m.; admission is free.

After the mission, it's time to get another giant taste of history. From Mission Road, go left onto Steves Avenue and right onto TX 536 Spur/Probandt Street. Take that to S. Alamo Street and go right until you reach **The Alamo** (300 Alamo Plaza; 210-225-1391; www.thealamo.org). This 4.2-acre complex was the site of the Battle of the Alamo, where a small group of Texans fought for thirteen days against the Centralist army of Gen. Antonio Lopez de Santa Anna until they were finally defeated on March 6, 1836. Visitors to the Alamo have access to various areas of the complex, such as a hospital, a church, military barracks, and a gift shop. Open 9 a.m. to 5:30 p.m. Mon through Sat and 10 a.m. to 5:30 p.m. Sun, although it sometimes closes later in summer months. Admission is free.

Now, go from one of San Antonio's most famous attractions to the next: the **River Walk** (210-227-4262; www.thesanantonio riverwalk.com). Simply cross Alamo Street and go down the stairs at any of the many River Walk access points. Lined with shops and restaurants, the 2-mile-long River Walk is a must-see for San Antonio visitors. Walk the banks, or hop on a boat for one of the thirty-five-minute narrated tours, which are offered 9 a.m. to 9 p.m. daily. Purchase tickets at various stations along the River Walk, or call (800) 417-4139 or visit www.riosanantonio.com to book.

DINNER Hopefully by now you're hungry, because you're in for a treat at **Boudro's Texas Bistro** (421 E. Commerce St.; 210-224-8484; www.boudros .com), which is known for having some of the best Tex-Mex and seafood in the state. The menu includes fare such as house-smoked shrimp and Gulf crab enchiladas, mesquite-grilled Texas quail, papaya-marinated Black Angus flank steak, and grilled portobello tostadas. Don't miss the incredible guacamole for two, made with diced avocado, roasted tomato and serrano peppers, cilantro, and fresh lime and orange juices and prepared tableside. Wash it down with a prickly pear margarita.

LODGING After a day of sightseeing, you're not going to want to do much driving, so walk or drive west on E. Commerce Street, go right on Soledad Street, and then turn left on E. Houston Street to the **Emily Morgan Hotel** (705 E. Houston St.; 210-225-5100; www.emilymorganhotel.com). Located right next to the Alamo, this luxury boutique hotel is known for its friendly staff and well-appointed rooms, which come with feather-top beds, 400-thread-count sheets, Jacuzzi tubs, and Aveda bath products. The hotel is nonsmoking and pet friendly. Be sure to ask for a room facing the Alamo grounds—the view is incredible. Check the website for rates and availability.

DAY 2/MORNING

BREAKFAST Go east on E. Houston Street to Bowie Street and go right. Then turn left onto E. Market Street and merge onto I-37 south/US 281 south to I-10. Take exit 138C toward Fair Avenue and take a slight right to Fair Avenue. Then, go right on S. Hackberry Street and end at **Patty's Taco House** (2422 S. Hackberry St.; 210-534-3395). This local favorite is known for quick and easy breakfast tacos in classic combinations such as bean and cheese, bacon and egg, and potato and egg. For the more adventurous, there's a super taco (ham, egg, potato, cheese, and bacon), a pork chop taco, and even a *lengua* (that's "tongue" in Spanish) version.

Next, go south on S. Hackberry Street to Steves Avenue and go right. Then, go left on TX 536 Spur south/Probandt Street and go left to I-10 west. Take that to US 90 west and merge onto Stotzer Freeway/TX 151 toward SeaWorld. Exit at Westover Hills Boulevard and turn left until it becomes SeaWorld Drive. **SeaWorld** (10500 SeaWorld Dr.; 210-523-3900; www.seaworld.com/sanantonio), a favorite San Antonio attraction, is an aqua-themed park with shows, rides, exhibits, and water parks, as well as behind-the-scenes tours and animal interaction programs. From watching a goofy sea lion show to suiting up and getting in the water with the gentle giants better known as beluga whales, if it concerns sea life, you can probably find it at SeaWorld. Tickets can get expensive, so check the website before you go for deals.

Then, go southeast on SeaWorld Drive and follow it until it becomes Westover Hills Boulevard. Turn right on TX 151 east/ Stotzer Freeway and go to exit I-410/TX 16 and then turn left onto the SW I-410 Loop. Follow I-410 north to US 281 south and take that toward I-37. Exit at Jones-Maltsberger Road and go left, then go right onto E. Basse Road until you reach the **Alamo Quarry Market** (255 E. Basse Rd.; 210-824-8885; www.quarrymarket.com). This shopping center is home to a host of great stores such as Ann Taylor, Banana Republic, Francesca's Collections, Lucchese Boot Co., Restoration Hardware, and Whole Earth Provision Co., as well as specialty shops such as Whole Foods Market, Woodhouse Day Spa, and Club Humidor.

LUNCH Once you've shopped up an appetite, head to **Papouli's Greek Grill** (located in the Quarry; 210-804-1118; www.papoulis.com), which serves up traditional and contemporary Greek food in a casual atmosphere. Menu items include gyros, spanikopita, pita sandwiches, Greek salad, avgolemono soup, and a variety of meat plates. Don't miss the jalapeño fire hummus or the falafel pita sandwich—both are menu standouts.

From there, take US 281 north to TPC Parkway and go right (this is about 2 miles north of Loop 1604). Then, go straight through the light at Bulverde Road and turn left at Marriott Parkway to the **JW Marriott San Antonio Hill Country** (23808 Resort Parkway; 210-403-3434; www.jwsanantonio.com), an upscale, 1,000-room resort that includes a spa, restaurants, water features, two golf courses, meeting facilities, and more. In addition to its atmosphere, which blends rustic decor from the Texas Hill Country with upscale, five-star accommodations and services, the resort has incorporated multiple green initiatives, such as close-in parking for low-emitting vehicles and "windricity" (wind power) that supplies the resort with 70 percent of what it needs.

Once you check in, head out to the **River Bluff Water Experience,** which features six acres of pools, waterfalls, rivers, lounges, and fountains that will entertain the entire family. Kids will love the winding, 1,200-foot lazy river ride, which wraps itself around the property, and the Acequia Tube Slides, which shoot daring water-lovers down 275 feet of twists and turns. Younger children will enjoy the children's pool with kiddie slides and spray features, as well as the zero-entry leisure pool that offers graduated access to the water. Looking for a more adult experience? Hang your hat at the Rivertop Grill, a full-service bar and restaurant that was modeled after the famous Gruene Hall. Grab a margarita or a draft beer and some Wahoo fish tacos and make your way out into the water—you won't regret it. Open from 8 a.m. to 10 p.m. daily.

Looking for a total adult experience? Try the **Lantana Spa,** a 26,000-square-foot facility that offers a full line of treatments as well as couples treatment suites, a private fitness studio, a spa bistro, and an adults-only pool with private cabanas. Signature treatments include a citrus blossom facial, Texas sarsaparilla and coffee scrub, river birch sports massage (great for golfers), a cattle baron's manicure for men, and a Texas wildflower footbath and massage for two. Call (210) 276-2300 for reservations.

Next, head to the **Crooked Branch Lobby Bar,** where a "sunset toast" is held daily at 6:30 p.m. Miss the toast? Guests of the resort also receive two welcome drinks upon arrival, which may be claimed in the bar. Grab a Titos and Sprite or a nice merlot and head out to a rocking chair on the sprawling patio, where the views of the Hill Country seem to go on for miles.

DINNER Hungry? Make a reservation at **Cibolo Moon**, the resort's primary restaurant, which serves up breakfast, lunch, and dinner with German and Mexican influences. Located in a beautifully decorated space, Cibolo Moon's menu includes options such as BBQ-grilled oysters, corn-fried green tomato salad with smoked mozzarella and cowboy candy relish, char-crusted rib eye, bison meat loaf with melted Brazos cheddar, and salt-and-pepper baby back ribs. The wide noodle pasta with pit-roasted chicken, mushrooms, and pancetta is to die for.

LODGING   A trip to the **JW Marriott San Antonio Hill Country** (23808 Resort Parkway; 210-403-3434; www.jwsanantonio.com) wouldn't be complete without an overnight stay, so, if you haven't already, book a room at the hotel, which uses aspects of Hill Country and San Antonio style (think tooled leather, cattle-hide furniture, and carved wood) to create a space that's both comfortable and luxurious. Standard rooms feature signature Marriott Revive beds, 37-inch LCD HD TVs, separate bathtubs and showers, and Hill Country views. Suites are also available.

DAY 3/MORNING

BREAKFAST   Before you hit the road for Houston, head back to **Cibolo Moon** to test out the breakfast offerings, which includes both a breakfast buffet (omelets, Belgian waffles, oatmeal, fruit, yogurt, breakfast breads, etc.) or individual selections such as a market vegetable scramble, a Texas-size pecan sticky bun, whole wheat crunchy French toast, and ranchers skillets with blends such as huevos rancheros, Mexican chorizo, refried beans, and fried eggs. Just make sure you also order coffee to get you through that drive home.

There's More . . . .

Fun. **San Antonio Raceway.** Quarter-mile drag racing track and school located near the city. 3641 Santa Clara Rd. in Marion; (210) 698-2310; www.sanantonioraceway.com.

   Six Flags Fiesta Texas. This 200-acre theme park is another family favorite, thanks to its attractions, rides, shows, and water park. 17000 I-10 west; (210) 697-5050; www.sixflags.com /fiestatexas.

   ZDT Amusement Center. Go-karts, parachute drop, rock wall, slide, giant trampoline, video games, and more. 1218 N. Camp St. in Seguin; (830) 386-0151; www.zdtamusement.com.

Kids. **Magik Children's Theatre.** A wonderful little theater that stages productions for kids year-round. 420 S. Alamo St.; (210) 227-2751; www.magiktheatre.org.

Museum. **San Antonio Museum of Art.** Permanent collections include Western antiquities, Asian art, Latin American art, and more. 200 W. Jones Ave.; (210) 978-8100; www.samuseum.org.

Shopping. **The Shops at La Cantera.** Open-air shopping, dining, and entertainment complex. 15900 La Cantera Parkway; (210) 582-6255; www.theshopsatlacantera.com.

Sports. **San Antonio Missions baseball.** Minor league baseball team with regular games and frequent specials such as $1 hot dog night. Nelson Wolff Stadium in San Antonio; (210) 675-7275; http://web.minorleaguebaseball.com.

San Antonio Spurs. NBA basketball held at AT&T Center. One AT&T Center; (210) 444-5000; www.nba.com/spurs.

Special Events & Festivals . . . .

APRIL

Fiesta San Antonio. Probably the most beloved tradition in San Antonio, this annual festival pays tribute to the city's history while raising money for today's organizations in need. Held at various venues; (210) 227-5191; www.fiesta-sa.org.

MAY

San Antonio New World Wine and Food Festival. A collection of wine and food tastings featuring local restaurants and wineries that are serving up some of the best fare in the region. (210) 822-9555; www.nwwff.org.

JUNE

San Antonio Film Festival. More than 120 independent films on three screens over five days. Held at the Instituto Cultural de Mexico in HemisFair Park, (210) 977-9004, www.safilm.com.

SEPTEMBER

International Photography Festival. A monthlong celebration that includes exhibits from around the world. www.fotoseptiembreusa .com.

Other Recommended Restaurants & Lodgings . . . . .

Acenar, 146 E. Houston St.; (210) 222-2362; www.acenar.com. Upscale Mexican bar and restaurant with a perfect location on the River Walk.

Alamo Café, 14250 San Pedro Ave.; (210) 495-2233; www.alamo cafe.com. Family-friendly joint with delicious margaritas and homemade tortillas.

Casarita Mexican Restaurant, 2895 Thousand Oaks Dr.; (210) 490-2726; www.casaritainc.com. Fantastic Tex-Mex and drinks in a laid-back atmosphere.

Crockett Hotel, 320 Bonham St.; (210) 225-6500; www.crockett hotel.com. Affordable yet nice hotel in the heart of downtown.

Drink Cocktail Bar, 200 Navarro at Market Street; (210) 224-1031; www.drinkcocktailbar.com. Huge mixed drink selection in a sexy atmosphere.

Grey Moss Inn, 19010 Scenic Loop Rd.; (210) 695-8301; www
.grey-moss-inn.com. Quality steaks, seafood, and comfort food in
a lovely location.

La Gloria Ice House, 100 E. Grayson; (210) 267-9040; www.lagloria
icehouse.com. Mexican restaurant and bar featuring street food,
ceviche, soups, tortas, and cocktails inspired by the South.

Omni La Mansion del Rio, 112 College St.; (210) 518-1000; www
.omnihotels.com. Upscale hotel chain located right on the River
Walk.

Sandbar Fish House and Market, 200 E. Grayson St.; (210) 222-
2426; www.pearlbrewery.com. Delicious seafood house located in
the Pearl Brewery complex.

For More Information . . . .

Comprehensive information about the city; www.sanantonio.com.

San Antonio Convention and Visitors Bureau; www.visitsanantonio
.com.

San Antonio Office of Cultural Affairs; www.sahearts.com.

NORTHBOUND
ESCAPES

NORTHBOUND ESCAPE *One*
The Woodlands
AN ESCAPE FROM THE CITY / 1 NIGHT

Fun for the kids
Golf
Shopping
Great restaurants
Natural setting

When time is of the essence, does it get any better than a fun-filled getaway that's just forty minutes outside of town? If you live in Houston, you're in luck, because the beautiful, well-preened master-planned community of The Wood-lands is just a quick hop up I-45.

A visit to the 62,000-population enclave is attractive for more reasons than its proximity, however: It's also entirely walkable and filled with plenty of attractions for all ages. In the past year alone The Woodlands has been listed among the country's top places to move, top shopping destinations, and top places to spend a weekend. The motto at Market Square, one of the town's popular shopping districts, is "enrich, enjoy, and escape," and a visit here will have you doing all three.

DAY 1/MORNING

From Houston, take I-45 north and exit Research Forest Drive in The Woodlands.

BREAKFAST Stop at **Black Walnut Café** (2520 Research Forest Dr.; 281-362-1678; www.blackwalnutcafe.com) for an incredible breakfast served starting at 6 a.m. on weekdays and 7 a.m. on weekends. Start with delectable berries and Chantilly crème or a handmade croissant, then graduate to a pico Benedict (poached eggs, spinach, and pico de gallo on an English muffin with house potatoes

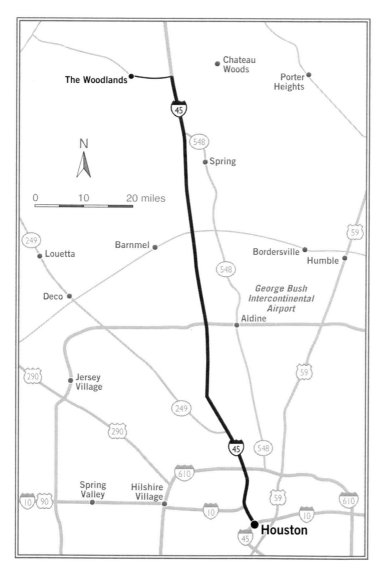

and cayenne citrus hollandaise), Texas-cut brioche French toast, or a roasted vegetable omelet.

Need something quick? Drop by **Taqueria Arandas** (25598 A I-45 north; 281-419-3582; www.taqueriasarandas.com) for two or three of their famous huevos rancheros or chilaquiles. Breakfast is served from 7 to 11 a.m. daily.

Next, hop back on the highway and head north toward **SplashTown** (21300 I-45 north; 281-355-3300; www.splashtownpark.com), a massive water park that's open Apr through Sept. Don't miss the Stingray Racer, a new slide complex with six waterslide lanes; the Texas Freefall, a five-story free-fall slide; the RipQurl, which takes riders on a hair-raising trip through the twists and turns of a dark tunnel; and the Big Spin, a crazy, funnel-shaped attraction. Look online in advance for discounts on admission; parking is free.

Then, get back on I-45 and merge onto Woodlands Parkway via exit 76B. Turn right on Waterway Avenue and park. Then, walk to the Woodlands Waterway Marriott Hotel and catch a ride on the **Woodlands Water Taxi** (281-367-1151; www.btd.org/Waterway .htm). You may not set any speed records, but a ride along the 1.4-mile waterway is a fun way to spend an hour and see The Woodlands from a new, duck's-eye-view vantage point. Even better, if you see something along the route you want to check out—the taxis go past popular shops, restaurants, and hotels—you can always hop off the boat and get back on again when you're ready. The taxis pick up at each of their twelve stops every forty-five to sixty minutes. An unlimited day pass is $5 for adults and $2.50 for youths, seniors, and the disabled. Open daily at 11 a.m.

Once you get back to the Marriott, disembark and walk around the corner to **Hubbell & Hudson** (24 Waterway Court; 281-203-5600; www.hubbellandhudson.com), a lovely little market/bistro featuring mouthwatering items such as fresh-baked jalapeño cheddar bread, slow-roasted potatoes, and pistachio mousse tart. The store also has a wide beer and wine selection—visitors are encouraged to "sip and shop"—and a floral department with colors spanning the rainbow. Take a look around, grab a latte from the coffee bar, and then head upstairs for a class with the **Viking Cooking School** (www.vikingcookingschool.com), where a quote on the wall by Anthelme Brillat Savarin commands, "Tell me what you eat and I will tell you who you are." Indeed, no matter what your pleasure, there's probably instruction for it at the school, which offers a variety of fun, educational classes on everything from knife skills to breakfast foods to cake decorating to planning a romantic dinner. Kids and teen classes are also available. Times, class lengths, and prices vary; call for details.

LUNCH If you are still hungry after your class, head next door to the **Hubbell & Hudson Bistro** (281-203-5641; www.hubbellandhudson.com/bistro), a new American bistro that serves lunch and dinner daily and brunch on Sat and Sun from 9 a.m. to 3 p.m. The bistro uses the freshest, in-season ingredients to dictate the menu, which changes frequently. Some year-round staples include pan-seared fois gras, seared sashimi, free-range chicken breast, pad thai, and cocktails from the full-service bar. Upscale yet casual, this is a great place to enjoy a lingering meal, particularly if you can grab a spot on the patio, which offers excellent people-watching.

AFTERNOON

You're in one of the area's shopping meccas, so it's worth dedicating an afternoon to at least browsing the huge variety of shops. Start on **Market Street** (bordered by Grogan's Mill, Lake Robbins, Six Pines, and Lake Woodlands; 281-419-4774; www.market street-thewoodlands.com), which encourages visitors to "shop all day, stay all night." Filled with stores, restaurants, and theaters, it is, indeed, a good place to spend at least a few hours. Among the many highlights: **Hemline** (9595 Six Pines, Suite 865; 281-292-1668; www.hemline.com), a women's boutique with trendy clothes and accessories; **Francesca's Collections** (9595 Six Pines, Suite 870; 281-419-3750; www.francescascollections.com), the perfect place to pick up a gift for your best girlfriend; **Swoozie's** (9595 Six Pines, Suite 810; 281-292-7666; www.swoozies.com), which has everything for your party needs; and **Luke's Locker** (9595 Six Pines, Suite 1060; 281-419-0326; www.lukeslocker.com), a one-stop shop for athletes of all types.

Next, head over the **Woodlands Mall** (1201 Lake Woodlands, Suite 700; 281-363-3409; www.thewoodlandsmall.com), which offers an additional range of shopportunities. The mall includes major retailers such as White House Black Market, Macy's, Forever 21, Anthropologie, Urban Outfitters, The Disney Store, BCBG Max Azria, Coach, Apple, and more, as well as a children's play area and carousel. It is also the site of more than a dozen restaurants such as the Cheesecake Factory, PF Chang's, Fleming's Steakhouse, and Rockfish Seafood Grill.

Now, head back outside and walk west on Lake Robbins Drive until you reach Town Green Park and the **Riva Row Boat House** (2101 Riva Row; 281-210-3965; www.thewoodlandstownship-tx .gov), a 1.6-acre park that rents single and tandem kayaks for use on the waterway. Cost is $15 for the first hour and $5 for each additional hour. Drink concessions and lockers are available.

Feeling exhausted from all of that kayaking? Head back to Market Street and pamper yourself with a treatment at **Bella Rinova Salon and Day Spa** (9595 Six Pines, Suite 1300; 713-554-5444; www.bellarinova.com), a full-service spa with treatments such as a signature aromatherapy facial, a "blueberry smoothie" facial peel, a desert heat body wrap, Swedish massage, and manicures and pedicures. For a decadent treat, try the caviar facial ($150), which uses protein-rich caviar to firm, tone, and hydrate your face. Seeking several treatments? Don't miss the full-day beautiful renewal package, which includes a salt glow, Italian river stone massage, an aromatherapy facial, makeup application, haircut and style, spa pedicure, spa manicure, and a spa lunch.

Traveling with kids? Include them in the spa experience with a trip to **Sweet & Sassy** (9595 Six Pines, Suite 530; 281-292-9090; www.sweetandsassy.com), a children's salon and spa offering haircuts, updos, hair braiding, and mini manicures and pedicures. Packages and hosted parties are also available. Want nothing but the best for your little princess? Try the Diva for a Day package, which includes a shampoo, haircut, style, mini mani and pedi, mini facial, makeup application, nail art, and a toe ring.

DINNER Once you're ready for dinner, stay in Market Street and head to **Grotto** (9595 Six Pines, Suite 100; 281-419-4252; www.grottohouston.com), which serves Old Country Italian cuisine such as meatballs with marinara, linguine with clam sauce, lobster bisque, sausage and pepper pizza, and chicken, veal, and eggplant Parmesan. Don't miss the delicious snapper Siciliano—capellini-crusted red snapper with jumbo lump crab and roma tomatoes in a garlic shrimp sauce, served with green beans and salad.

NIGHTLIFE After dinner, walk south on Six Pines to Lake Robbins and catch a show at the **Cynthia Woods Mitchell Pavilion** (2005 Lake Robbins; 281-363-3300; www.woodlandscenter.org), an open-air, outdoor amphitheater that brings in the best musicians and bands, such as the Dave Matthews Band, Jimmy Buffet, and Sheryl Crow, from around the country. Spread out a blanket on the grassy hill, order a beer, and get ready for a tunes-filled night under the stars.

In the mood for a little more action? Take Lake Robbins Drive east to I-45 and go north to The Woodland's **Main Event** (19441 I-45 south; 281-355-5511; www.maineventusa.net), which offers fun for the whole family with activities such as bowling, rock climbing, billiards, laser tag, glow golf, and more.

LODGING For an experience that will take your mind far away from Houston, head back to Market Street for a night or two at the beautiful, glamorous **Avia Hotel** (9595 Six Pines, Suite 1100; 281-203-5005; www.aviahotels.com), which opened in The Woodlands in December 2009. From the spiral staircase in the lobby to the glittering crystals that hang over the check-in desk, this place radiates luxury. The hotel's seventy rooms include amenities such as Dean & Deluca snacks, 42-inch flat-panel TVs, free Wi-Fi, Simmons mattresses, and waffle terry robes. Don't miss the sparkling infinity pool, either, which overlooks Market Street.

DAY 2/MORNING

BREAKFAST Once you've caught up on your sleep, head over to **Jasper's** (9595 Six Pines, Suite 900; 281-298-6600; www.kentrathbun.com/jaspers). Known for its "gourmet backyard cuisine," Jasper's serves upscale American home cooking and offers a unique brunch on Sat and Sun from 11 a.m. to 3 p.m. Signature brunch items include vanilla French toast, a white truffle and aged Gouda omelet, wood-grilled flat-iron steak and eggs, and prosciutto-wrapped shrimp 'n' grits. Can't make it for brunch? The restaurant also offers a fantastic happy hour Mon through Sat from open to 7 p.m. and from 9 p.m. to close and all day on Sun that includes a selection of $5 cocktails such as a dirty blue martini and $5 edibles such as herb-fried goat cheese with crostini. Don't miss the fantastic carne guisada flautas.

Next, work off that brunch with a round of golf at one of the many courses in The Woodlands. One favorite public course is **Oaks Golf Course** at The Woodlands Resort & Conference Center (2301 N. Millbend; 281-882-3000; www.woodlandsresort.com), which features oak-lined fairways, 4,500-square-foot greens, and a full-service pro shop. The Oaks' sister course, **Panther Trail Golf Course** (2301 N. Millbend; 281-882-3000; www.woodlandsresort.com), is another solid option with four tee placements on each hole, innovative course contours, and interesting water features.

If you're traveling with the kids, make a visit to Market Street's **Waterway Square** (31 Waterway Square Place; 281-363-2447; www.thewoodlandscvb.com), a one-acre public plaza that features a synchronized musical fountain and interactive fountain for kids to play in.

LUNCH Walk west along the waterway until you reach the **Goose's Acre Bistro and Irish Pub** (21 Waterway Ave.; 281-466-1502; www.thegoosesacre.com), an authentic Irish restaurant and bar. The decor inside was brought over from a bar in Midleton, Ireland, that was forced to close in 2005, by owners Brian Young and Colm O'Neill. The menu features Irish favorites such as cod fish and chips, corned beef and cabbage, and sirloin shepherd's pie, as well as American favorites like fried mozzarella sticks, barbecue beef back ribs, and build-your-own pizza.

After lunch, walk toward Market Street for dessert at **Red Mango** (9595 Six Pines, Suite 1250; 281-419-7774; www.redmangousa.com), which serves low-cal frozen yogurt made with live and active cultures to promote digestive health.

There's More . . . .

Sightseeing. **Woodlands Waterway Trolley.** Free trolley that takes visitors to major Woodlands' attractions such as Waterway Square, the Cynthia Woods Mitchell Pavilion, and Town Green Park. (979) 778-0607; www.thewoodlandscvb.com/trolley.

Sports. **AMF Woodlands Lanes.** Bowling lanes with food and drinks. 27000 I-45 north in Conroe; (281) 367-1277; www.amf.com.

Gator Motorplex. A quarter-mile oval high-banked race track offering races every Sat at 7 p.m. 14350 Old US 75 in Willis; (936) 588-6127; www.gatormotorplex.net.

Shankz Black Light Miniature Golf. Minigolf course with black-light features. 3091 College Park Dr.; (936) 273-4569; www.shankzgolf.com.

Theater. **Tinseltown 17 at The Woodlands.** Cinema with multiple screens featuring the hottest new releases. 1600 Lake Robbins; (281) 362-4340; www.cinemark.com.

Town Center Theatre offers various performances including summer musicals. 3800 S. Panther Creek; (832) 592-9697.

The Woodlands Repertory Theatre. Pre-professional theater with acting opportunities for all ages. (936) 273-3395; www .thewoodlandsrep.org.

Special Events & Festivals . . . .

JANUARY

Taste of the Town. Community event featuring food from more than seventy area restaurants. (281) 367-5777; www.tasteofthetown.org.

APRIL

The Woodlands Waterway Arts Festival. An annual festival held in Town Center with more than 200 national and regional artists selling their creations. Proceeds benefit local charities. (281) 507-0343; www.woodlandsartsfestival.com.

MAY

The Woodland's Women's Show. Held at Waterway Marriott Hotel & Convention Center, the event features items for sale, such as clothes, accessories and purses, gourmet treats, and makeovers. www.thewoodlandswomensshow.com.

JUNE

Wine & Food Week. An annual celebration of food and wine featuring famous chefs from around the country and more than 500 wines. Held at various spots in town. (713) 557-5732; www .wineandfoodweek.com.

AUGUST

Fall Home & Garden Show. An annual show held at The Woodlands Waterway Marriott Hotel & Convention Center. www.woodlands shows.com.

NOVEMBER

Children's Festival. An annual festival celebrating children at the Cynthia Woods Mitchell Pavilion. (281) 363-3300; www.woodlands center.org.

Other Recommended Restaurants & Lodgings . . . . .

Berripop, 25 Waterway Court; (281) 419-8484; www.berripop .com. Popular frozen yogurt spot.

Chuy's, 18035 I-45 at Research Forest in Shenandoah; (936) 321-4440; www.chuys.com. Quirky, delicious Tex-Mex and margaritas.

Courtyard by Marriott, 1020 Lake Front Circle; (281) 292-3262; www.marriott.com.

CRU, 9595 Six Pines, Suite 650; (281) 465-9463; www.cru awinebar.com. Wine bar serving lunch, cheese plates, and dinner entrees.

Crush Wine Lounge, 20 Waterway Court; (281) 362-7874; www .thecrushbar.com. Popular wine bar that also serves food.

Fairfield Inn & Suites, 16850 I-45 south; (936) 271-0110; www .marriott.com.

Freebirds, 1640 Lake Woodlands; (281) 419-8011; www.freebirds .com. Huge, filling burritos in all makes and models.

Hilton Garden Inn, 9301 Six Pines; (281) 364-9301; hiltongarden inn.hilton.com.

Nit Noi, 6700 Woodlands Parkway, Suite 250; (281) 367-3355; www.nitnoithai.com. Thai restaurant and cafe.

Residence Inn, 1040 Lake Front Circle; (281) 292-3252; www .marriott.com.

Tesar's, 1701 Lake Robbins; (281) 465-0700; www.tesarsthe woodlands.com. Steak and seafood served in a modern atmosphere.

Tommy Bahama's Tropical Café, 9595 Six Pines, Suite 700; (281) 292-8669; www.tommybahama.com. Like the famous shirts, the menu here is tropical. Think pineapple, crab, and coconut shrimp.

Uni Sushi, 9595 Six Pines, Suite 860; (281) 298-7177; www .unisushiwoodlands.com. Regularly voted the best sushi in The Woodlands.

The Woodlands Resort & Conference Center, 2301 North Millbend Dr.; (281) 367-1100; www.woodlandsresort.com. Popular hotel with golf and water activities.

The Woodlands Waterway Marriott Hotel & Convention Center, 1601 Lake Robbins; (281) 367-9797; www.marriott.com. Upscale hotel with spa, restaurants, and convenient access to other Woodlands locations.

For More Information . . . .

The Woodlands Chamber of Commerce; www.woodlandschamber .org.

The Woodlands Convention and Visitors Bureau; www.thewoodlands cvb.com.

Woodlands living; www.thewoodlands.com.

NORTHBOUND ESCAPE *Two*
Huntsville
UNLOCKING HISTORY—AND GOING BEHIND BARS—IN
HUNTSVILLE / 1 NIGHT

Natural attractions
Texas history
Prison tourism
College town
Shopping
Down-home food

Nestled in the heart of East Texas's Piney Woods, the first thing that strikes you about Huntsville is how green it is. Bordered by expansive forests and parks, the town is a can't-miss for nature lovers who will enjoy hiking its trails, camping under towering trees, and taking a dip in area lakes.

The town is best known, however, for other reasons, the first of which greets you in the form of a giant statue the minute you get into town: Sam Houston. Huntsville was the home and is the resting place of Houston, who served as president of the Republic of Texas and governor of the state of Texas. Around town, you'll find plenty of things named for him, including Sam Houston State University, which infuses a fresh vibe into this city.

And of course you can't forget Huntsville's other claim to fame as the home of Texas's execution chamber. Rather than shunning this distinction, Huntsville embraces it, offering prison- and inmate-themed tourism throughout town.

Whether you go for a hike, a walk back in time, or a photo op behind bars, Huntsville will offer you a fun, quick weekend escape.

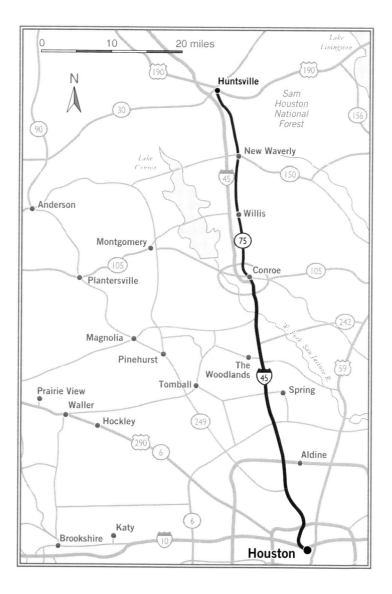

DAY 1/MORNING

From Houston, take I-45 north for about 70 miles until you reach Huntsville. The giant Sam Houston statue will let you know that you've arrived.

Make a pit stop at the **National Museum of Funeral History** (415 Barren Springs Dr. off I-45 north at exit 64; 281-876-3063; www.nmfh.org), which is home to a macabre but fascinating collection of death-related artifacts including a re-created casket factory, an exhibit on Civil War embalming, and a selection of "fantasy coffins" shaped like a Mercedes Benz, a fishing canoe, and a shallot.

BREAKFAST From I-45, go right on TX 75 into town and go right on Sam Houston Avenue, where you'll see the **Donut Wheel** (1223 Sam Houston Ave.; 936-291-0892), an old-fashioned doughnut shop serving up classics such as bear claws, kolaches, glazed twists, cake doughnuts, doughnut holes, and more. The best part? My two doughnuts and two doughnut holes cost less than $2. Open Mon through Fri from 4 a.m. to 4 p.m. and Sat and Sun from 4 a.m. to 2 p.m.

Craving something a little heartier? Just up the street, **Lindo Mexico Taqueria** (902 11th St.; 936-293-8040) has a full selection of Tex-Mex offerings including fantastic, dirt-cheap breakfast tacos. The lunch and dinner prices are average, though.

Once you've fueled up, head west on TX 75 back to I-45 south to Park Road 40 and go right to **Huntsville State Park** (Park Road 40; 936-295-5644; www.tpwd.state.tx.us). This wooded park offers activities such as camping, hiking, boating, swimming, fishing, Hydrobike rentals, nature study, and biking. Call ahead to set up an hourlong guided horseback trail ride or an "eat and ride" breakfast or dinner ride at the on-site **Lake Raven Stables** (936-295-1985). Admission is $4 a day for ages 13 and up.

Head back to I-45 and follow signs for the **Sam Houston Statue Visitors Center and Gift Shop** (7600 TX 75 south; 936-291-9726;

www.huntsvilletexas.com), where you can learn all about the approximately 65-foot-tall "Big Sam" statue and other tourist attractions in the area. Created by artist David Adickes, who used sixty tons of concrete and steel to make the monument, Big Sam is the world's tallest statue of an American hero. Even if you've seen it from the highway, it's definitely worth a stop to see it up close, as details such as the handcrafted buttons on his vest and the dimple in his chin take on a new dimension. After you've snapped some photos, stop by the gift shop for your fill of arts and crafts such as Texas-size jelly beans, Dr Pepper beef jerky, miniature branding irons, and barbecue cookbooks. Across the hall, the visitor center is stocked with information about other area attractions. Admission is free.

Now, get back on I-45 north and go 4 miles until you hit exit 118 and follow signs for the **Texas Prison Museum** (491 TX 75 north; 936-295-2155; www.txprisonmuseum.org). Among the most fascinating museums I've ever been to, the Texas Prison Museum—which is a nonprofit—is best known for being home to "Old Sparky," the Texas electric chair where 361 men died between 1924 and 1964. Other items of note include a history of Death Row at the "Walls Unit," a display of actual confiscated weapons including a ball made of paint chips placed in a sock as a bludgeon, an exhibit about famous inmates such as David Crosby and John Wesley Hardin, and a re-created cell where, for $3, you can get your picture taken wearing prison stripes.

LUNCH Drive through town until you reach the corner of 14th Avenue and Avenue J. When you see a parking lot filled with cars, you'll know you've found **Farmhouse Café** (1004 14th St.; 936-435-1450; www.farmhousecafe.net), one of the best restaurants in Huntsville. With its fresh, down-home food and friendly staff, you can't go wrong with lunch at this place. Signature dishes include the blue-plate special, which changes daily and comes with two sides, as well as pepper fried steak and the classic club. And if you go when fried green tomatoes are in season, be sure to order those, too.

Want something a little more upscale? Go three blocks over to **Junction** (2641 11th St.; 936-291-2183), a steak and seafood restaurant set in a plantation home. Grab a seat upstairs and order the prime rib and shrimp. You won't be disappointed.

AFTERNOON

After lunch, head east on 11th Street and take a left on Avenue I until you reach **Oakwood Cemetery** (9th Street and Avenue I; 936-295-8113), the self-chosen grave where Sam Houston was laid to rest after dying from pneumonia in 1863. "The world will take care of Houston's fame," reads a quote by Andrew Jackson on the grave's facade, which is located on the west end of the cemetery. After you pay your respects, take some time to wander the rest of the cemetery, which features graves of all shapes and sizes, including some so worn you can barely read their inscriptions.

Now, switch gears (literally) by hopping in the car for a **prison driving tour** created by the Huntsville Convention and Visitors Bureau. Pick up a copy of the tour at the bureau or the statue visitor center, or follow these loose directions. The tour centers around the area between 11th and 14th Streets and Avenue J and Avenue G. It may seem odd for a town like Huntsville to so fully embrace that aspect of its identity, but when you visit, you'll see why it works. The walls, cells, and history of this place are so fascinating you can't help but want to know more. Some highlights include the Huntsville "Walls Unit," which is the oldest operating Texas prison (815 12th St.); the sprawling former director's residence (1206 Avenue I); the gravestone of Chief Santana, a Kiowa Indian chieftain convicted of killing seven white settlers in the 1871 Salt Creek Massacre (13th Street and Avenue I); and the Death House, where Texas's Death Row inmates are executed (corner of 12th Street and Avenue I).

Next, spend some time visiting other historic sites. Downtown, **Cabin on the Square** (1105 University Ave.; 936-435-1091) offers a neat glimpse of an 1800s-era structure that functioned as everything from a single-family home to a rental property to a hay storage shed. Open Thurs through Sat from 10 a.m. to 2 p.m. Admission is free. Then, head down the street to the **Gibbs-Powell Home Museum** (1228 11th St.; 936-294-0057), an immaculate, Greek Revival–style home built by the Gibbs-Powell family, which was close friends with Sam Houston. Open Thurs through Sun from 2 to 5 p.m. Admission is $3 for adults, free for children.

Round out your visit with some shopping along Courthouse Square, where the boutiques, antiques shops, and gift stores are sure to catch your fancy. If you're into antiquing, don't miss **Callie Magee Antiques** (1118 11th St.; 936-295-4501), **Bluebonnet Square Antiques** (1110 11th St.; 936-291-2800), and **Sam Houston Antique Mall** (1210 Sam Houston Ave.; 936-295-7716). Favorite boutiques include **Lisa's Gift Box** (1103 12th St.; 936-295-0892), **The Yarn Bar** (1111 12th St.; 936-291-9400), **Audie's Boutique** (1109 12th St.; 936-293-1516), and **FarmHouse Sweets and Eats** (1112 11th St.; 936-291-6988).

DINNER From the square, take a left on Sam Houston Avenue until you get to **Humphrey's** (1930 Sam Houston Ave.; 936-439-0664; www.jollyfoxclub .com), a bar and grill featuring solid pub grub, a wonderful outside patio, and cheap pitchers of beer. Live music is frequently featured on weekends. Try the chicken club sandwich.

Not in the mood for the bar scene? Instead, head back to I-45 to **Margarita's** (630 I-45 south; 936-293-8966; www.margaritashuntsville.com), a laid-back Tex-Mex joint with solid food and fantastic margaritas (hence the name). Don't miss the Lupe's loaded queso, the Mexican gumbo, or the "Golden Burrito."

NIGHTLIFE Huntsville may be small, but it's also a college town, so if you want somewhere to grab a nightcap, you do have a few options, the best of which is **Stardust Room** (1115 University Ave.; 936-293-1295), a fun venue with food, good drinks, and live music.

LODGING Huntsville's lodging options consist primarily of chain hotels, but if you want something unique and beautiful, look to the **Whistler Bed and Breakfast** (906 Avenue M; 936-295-2834; www.thewhistlerbnb.com). This charming B&B set in a historic, neoclassical family home is conveniently located next to downtown and radiates a calm, Southern vibe. Think wide front porch, relaxing swings, Tiffany lamps, and homey yet classic furniture.

DAY 2/MORNING

BREAKFAST The **Whistler Bed and Breakfast** serves a fantastic full Southern breakfast.

Or head to **Café Texan** (1120 Sam Houston Ave.; 936-295-2381), which also serves a variety of Southern specialties. Don't miss the biscuits and gravy.

Now, take I-45 south to Pinedale Road and go left until you reach **The Blue Lagoon** (649 Pinedale Rd.; 936-438-8888; www.bluelagoonscuba.net) for a scuba lesson. An incredible dive facility featuring fresh, turquoise water surrounded by pine trees, this will definitely be a memorable experience for you. Call ahead to set up a class.

Once you've dried off, head back to I-45 to **Ravens Nest Golf Course** (457 I-45 south; 936-438-8588; www.ravennestgolf.com), a multiuse eighteen-hole course set in the heart of the woods with native trees, creeks, and wildlife around every corner. Named one of the best economy courses in Texas, greens fees for eighteen holes are $23; discounts are available for Sam Houston State University students and alumni.

LUNCH Feeling like something exotic? Take I-45 north to TX 75 north and stop at **Puerto Aventura International Cuisine** (269 TX 75 north, Suite C; 936-435-0258; www.puertoaventurarestaurant.com), which specializes in a mix of Colombian, Cuban, and Greek cuisines. Specialties include a tender Cuban sandwich and fully loaded Greek gyro. Entrees start around $11. Open Mon through Sat from 11 a.m. to 9 p.m. Closed on Sun.

Now it's time to head back to Houston, but not before making a pit stop in Conroe. Take I-45 south to FM 3083 and go west to reach the **Southern Star Brewing Company** (1207 N. FM 3083 east in Conroe; 936-441-2739; www.southernstarbrewery.com), located inside a 10,000-square-foot warehouse. Founded in March 2008, the brewery now distributes its beers, including the popular Buried Hatchet and Bombshell Blonde, in Houston, Dallas, Austin, San Antonio, and College Station. Tours are held Sat at 1 p.m. Admission is free.

There's More . . . .

History. **Sam Houston State University Campus.** Nearly 17,000 students attend this attractive university. The visitor center is located at 1903 University Ave.; (936) 294-1844; www.shsu.edu.

    Samuel Walker Houston Cultural Center. Dedicated to the prominent black Walker County educator, the center contains a variety of informative exhibits. 1604 10th St.; (936) 295-2119.

Museum. **Sam Houston Memorial Museum and Park Complex.** The ultimate resource on all things related to Sam Houston's life and times. 1402 19th St.; (936) 294-1832; www.shsu.edu/~smm.

Shopping. **West Hill Mall.** Chain and unique shopping. 2 Financial Plaza; (936) 295-8268; www.westhillmall.com.

Sports. Huntsville Lanes. Popular bowling alley among students and locals. 663 I-45 south; (936) 295-3267; www.huntsvillelanes .com.

Special Events & Festivals . . . .

MARCH
General Sam Houston's Birthday and Texas Independence Celebration, Huntsville. Celebratory activities held at the Sam Houston Museum and Oakwood Cemetery. (936) 294-1832; www.sam houston.memorial.museum.

Walker County Fair, Rodeo, and Barbecue Cookoff, Huntsville. Cook-off, rodeo events, livestock, carnival, contests, and more. (936) 291-8763.

APRIL
General Sam Houston Folk Festival, Huntsville. Celebration of Sam Houston featuring nineteenth-century dress, life-skill demonstrations, children's activities, and entertainment. (936) 294-1832; www.samhoustonfolkfestival.org.

Herb Festival, Huntsville. Breads, herbs, plants, and more on sale. Hosted by the Garden Club, the event is held on City Hall grounds. (936) 436-1017.

MAY
Annual Airing of the Quilts, Huntsville. More than 300 quilts for display and sale throughout downtown. (936) 295-8322; www.tall pinesquiltguild.com.

OCTOBER

Fair on the Square, Huntsville. Arts and crafts show featuring entertainment in the downtown square. (936) 295-8113; www.chamber .huntsville.tx.us.

Other Recommended Restaurants & Lodgings . . . . .

HUNTSVILLE

Days Inn and Suites, 160 I-45 south; (936) 438 8400; www.days inn.com.

The Dodge Getaway Bed and Breakfast, 89 Dodge Oakhurst Rd.; (936) 295-1245; www.thedodgegetaway.com.

Fat Boys, 1932 Sam Houston Ave.; (936) 295-3902. Great burgers and beers.

Holiday Inn Express, 148 S. I-45 south; (936) 295-4300; www .ichotelsgroup.com.

Lizards Billiards and Grill, 1231 Josey St.; (936) 435-9111. Solid food and fun nightlife.

Oak View Manor Bed and Breakfast, 7137 TX 75 south; (936) 295-3352; www.oakviewmanorbnb.com.

Sam Houston State University Hotel, 1610 Bobby K. Marks Dr.; (936) 291-2151; www.shsuhotel.org.

LAKE LIVINGSTON

Bethy Creek Resort, FM 980 East Riverside in Lake Livingston; (936) 594-2511; www.bethycreek.com.

For More Information . . . .

City information; www.huntsvilletx.gov.

General info; www.huntsvilletexas.com.

Huntsville Chamber of Commerce; www.chamber.huntsville.tx.us.

Walker County information; www.co.walker.tx.us.

NORTHBOUND ESCAPE *Three*
Waco Area
DEFYING THE STEREOTYPES IN WACO / 1 NIGHT

It's hard to find a place in Texas with a weirder reputation than Waco. After all, it was home to the Branch Davidians, the religious sect that initiated a standoff with the FBI in 1993 resulting in the death of eighty members of the group and four federal agents. It's

- Dr Pepper Museum
- Parks
- Water activities
- Wineries
- Unique dining

also the home of Baylor University, a private Baptist University known for its strict regulations.

But beyond any preconceptions, Waco, a city with a population of about 120,000, is also home to wonderful, interesting attractions that make it a nice destination for a weekend away. Located about three hours from Houston, your weekend here will be something you'll be talking about well into the workweek.

DAY 1/MORNING

From Houston, take US 290 west to TX 6 north and stay on that for about 120 miles.

ON THE WAY Stop in Navasota to visit the **World's Largest Teapot** (8101 TX 6; 936-825-7400). Located at Martha's Bloomers Home and Garden Store, the giant white teapot is decorated with flowers and offers the perfect pit stop photo op. If you have time, stick around for some tea and a slice of delectable cobbler.

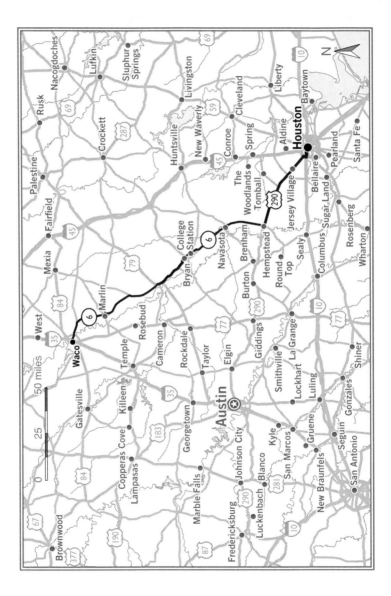

BREAKFAST Once you get to town, exit to TX 396/Bosque Boulevard and go right until you reach **Cappuccino Café** (4700 Bosque Blvd.; 254-772-3739; www .cafecappuccinotexas.com), a favorite breakfast joint with a full espresso bar and packed menu featuring omelets, breakfast quesadillas, French toast, pancakes, waffles, and more. Don't miss the spicy hot link sausage omelet with onion and cheddar cheese or the popular banana nut French toast, which is made with home-made banana bread. Open daily at 6 a.m. except Sun, when it opens at 7:30 a.m.

After breakfast, go northeast on Bosque Boulevard and take a right on 26th Street, then go left on US 84 east and right on N. University Parks Drive until you reach the 416-acre **Cameron Park** (University Parks Drive and Martin Luther King Drive along the Brazos River; 254-750-5980). Filled with winding trails, water features, and green expanses, Cameron Park is just the place to show you how beautiful Waco can be. While you're there, play a round of disc golf, hit the trails on your mountain bike, or even hit the Brazos River for some canoeing or kayaking. The park is free and open year-round.

Next, go northwest on University Parks Drive, left on US 84 and right on N. 4th Street until you reach **Cameron Park Zoo** (1701 N. 4th St.; 254-750-8400; www.cameronparkzoo.com). Packing quite a punch, this small zoo that opened in 1993 offers every-thing from an African lion display to a herpetarium to a Texas ranch house from the 1880s. Featured animals come from Africa, South America, North America, Asia, and Madagascar. The zero-depth splash fountain is great for the little ones, and the Brazos River exhibit provides a history lesson for all ages. Don't miss Lemur Island, where Sclater's black lemur—an endangered species found in only fourteen zoos worldwide—can be studied. And be sure to take your time here—the calm, spacious layout of the zoo makes it perfect for lingering. Opens at 9 a.m. Mon through Sat and 11 a.m. Sun. Tickets are $9 for adults, $8 for seniors 60 and up, $6 for kids 4–12, and free for kids under 4.

LUNCH After the zoo, take a right on Garland Avenue and take that to N. 5th Street; go left. Take that until you reach Austin Avenue and go left until you see the **Olive Branch Bakery and Café** (330 Austin Ave.; 254-757-0885; www.olive branchwaco.com), which opened in 2003 in hopes of feeding the bevy of hungry students regularly traipsing through town looking for a solid lunch. Offerings here include sandwiches, salads, pastas, and quiches. Be sure to try the create-your-own pasta and the soup, served in a fresh-baked bread bowl.

AFTERNOON

Spend the early afternoon hopping around Waco's museums, which are surprisingly interesting and diverse. Start at the **Texas Ranger Hall of Fame & Museum** (I-35 Frontage Road and S. University Parks Drive; 254-750-8631; www.texasranger.org). This is the official museum of the Texas Rangers, who played a vital role as law enforcers in Texas beginning in the 1800s. In addition to offering an interesting history of the Rangers, the museum is home to a Hall of Fame that pays tribute to those who died in the line of duty. Admission is $6 for adults, $3 for children 6–12, and free for children under 6.

Next, head down the street to the **Mayborn Museum Complex** (1300 S. University Parks Dr.; 254-710-1110; www.mayborn museum.com), a family-friendly museum with a variety of exhibits including Waco at the Crossroads of Texas, which features a walk-in diorama of a limestone cave, a Comanche tepee, and a Waco Mammoth section that includes a re-creation of Columbian mammoth bones unearthed 5 miles away at the Waco Mammoth site at Baylor University. Don't miss the amazing 28-foot-long model of a pliosaur, a big-toothed carnivorous sea monster. Opens daily at 10 a.m. except Sun, when it opens at 1 p.m. Admission is $6 for adults, $5 for seniors 65 and over, and $4 for children.

Finally, lighten things up by going northwest on S. University Parks Drive until you reach Mary Avenue and go left. Stop when you reach 5th Street and see the **Dr Pepper Museum** (300 S. 5th St.; 254-757-1025; www.drpeppermuseum.com). Any trip to Waco wouldn't be complete without a trip to this fun little museum filled with interesting artifacts such as early bottling equipment, the first Dr Pepper bottles, and a 1924 pickup truck that's part of an exhibit on rural general stores. Hourlong tours, which include the story of Dr Pepper, a visit to the bottling room, and other on site exhibits and samples from the soda fountain, are $5 and are available by reservation.

Once you've gotten your fill of soda, take time to sample another beverage in Waco: wine. Start by going east on 5th Street until you reach S. University Parks Drive and go right. Then, go left on US 77 Business Route and right onto TX 484 Spur south until it becomes TX 6. End at **Tehuacana Creek Vineyards and Winery** (6826 E. TX 6; 254-875-2375; www.wacowinery.com), a family-owned and -operated winery in Waco since 1997. The more than 1,300 vines on the property produce delicious white and red blends including its fruity Plantation White, the hearty Norton, and the light Heart of Texas Rose. Free tours and tastings are offered Mon through Thurs from noon to 5 p.m., Fri from noon to 6 p.m., and Sat from 10 a.m. to 6 p.m.

DINNER Now that you've tasted, take TX 6 west to US 77 BR and go left until it becomes La Salle Avenue. Take that until you see the exit for TX 396/ Valley Mills Drive and get on S. Valley Mills Drive until you see **Elite Circle Grille** (2132 South Valley Mills Dr.; 254-754-4941; www.elitecirclegrille.com), one of the best restaurants in Waco. Featuring a classic feel with a very current menu, the Elite is the perfect place for a filling dinner. Menu favorites include Shiner Bock–battered onion rings, coconut shrimp, the Elite chili cheeseburger, BBQ baby back ribs, and a twelve-ounce New York Strip. And don't miss the flavorful Asian lettuce wraps, divine hot and crunchy trout—cornflake-crusted ruby trout with jalapeño jelly sauce, texmati rice, and grilled veggies—or the melt-in-your-mouth white chocolate espresso cream custard.

NIGHTLIFE Wrap up the night by heading west on S. Valley Mills Drive to I-35 north and going left. Turn left on S. University Parks Drive and left on Mary Avenue until you see **Wild West Waco** (115 Mary St.; 254-759-1081; www.wildwest waco.com), one of the most popular late-night joints in the city. With more than 12,000 square feet of dance space, this bar/dance hall regularly packs the floor with dancers eager to two-step their way well into the night. Nightly drink specials are another draw, as is the fun mix of people who visit the club.

Sound too high-impact for you? Then make your way instead to the **Last Drive-in Picture Show** (2912 S. TX 36 in Gatesville; 254-865-8445), a classic drive-in movie theater that opened in 1950 and shows the hottest new releases. Charges are per car, and the snack bar is well stocked for those late-night munchies.

LODGING Want a great place to rest your head? After your night out, go south on Mary Avenue until you reach 20th Street and go right. When you see Austin Avenue, go right again and stop at the **Cotton Palace Bed and Breakfast** (1910 Austin Ave.; 254-753-7294; www.thecottonpalace.com), a modern yet charming B&B that has become an institution in Waco. Featuring updated rooms, fine bedding, and whirlpool tubs, the Cotton Palace manages to be both quaint and comfortable. Don't miss the complimentary beverages and the bottomless cookie jar.

Or, for a real taste of the country, head 20 miles out of town to **Moon River Ranch** (254-546-2233; www.moonriverranch.com), a gorgeous complex that offers two buildings—the Farmhouse and the Boathouse—for use by guests. In addition to the beautiful setting, all guests receive a golf cart during their stay and a private, self-serve gourmet breakfast. A two-night minimum stay is required.

DAY 2/MORNING

BREAKFAST The Cotton Palace serves a full, gourmet breakfast daily in the red dining room that includes fresh brewed Costa Rican coffee, tea or juices, seasonal fruit in champagne wine sauce, crème brûlée French toast, green chile strata, and lemon soufflé pancakes.

Want something off premises? Try the **Harold Waite Pancake and Steak House** (941 Lake Air Dr.; 254-772-9970), which is known among locals for its solid, cheap breakfast offerings. Be warned, though—they only accept cash.

Next, take Austin Avenue south until you hit Valley Mills Drive; go right and follow that until you reach **Waco Lake** (254-756-5359; www.swf-wc.usace.army.mil/waco), a sparkling lake with 79,000 acre-feet of water operated by the U.S. Army Corps of Engineers that offers fishing, hike and bike trails, camping, day-use areas, boating, swimming, horseback riding, and more.

While you're at the lake, stop by **Airport Beach** (on the north shore of the lake just west of the dam; 254-756-5359; www .swf-wc.usace.army.mil/waco). This park offers a sandy beach perfect for families as well as a playground, shelter area, picnic sites, and a boat ramp. Entry fee is $4 per vehicle.

Since you're in the neighborhood, drop by **Lakeside Tavern** (6605 Airport Rd.; 254-756-0399), a great little dive bar located next to Airport Beach. From the outside it looks fairly bland, but on the inside you'll find live music, cold beers, and lively company. Open until 2 a.m. nightly.

Still in your swimsuit? Go northwest on Airport Road and right on FM 3051. Take that to N. 19th Street and go right, then turn left on Lake Shore Drive until you reach **Waco Water Park** (900 W. Lake Shore Dr.; 254-750-7900; www.texastravelstop.com). Operated by the City of Waco, this park is particularly attractive to children, who will love its waterslides, pools, toys, and more.

LUNCH It may sound like a dieter's dream, but there's nothing healthy about **Health Camp** (2601 Circle Rd.; 254-752-2081), a burger joint located off the Waco Traffic Circle near I-35. Still, the fare here is worth the calories, from the Super Healthburger (consisting of two meat patties, two slices of cheese, and slathered in special sauce) to the creamy, decadent butterscotch shakes.

AFTERNOON

After lunch, take I-35 north to University Parks Drive and go left until you reach the **Waco Suspension Bridge** (at University Parks Drive between Franklin and Washington Avenues; 254-750-8080). When it was finished in 1870, this single-span suspension bridge was the longest of its kind west of the Mississippi. Fun fact: The cable used to build the bridge was supplied by John Roebling Co., the same company that built the Brooklyn Bridge. Admission to the bridge is free.

Next, go southeast on University Parks Drive, then right on Clay Avenue, then left on S. 4th Street. End at the **Earle-Napier-Kinnard House** (814 S. 4th St.; 254-753-5266; www.historicwaco .org/enk.htm), a Greek revival house built in 1858 that is said to be the second brick house built in Waco. Open weekends from 2 to 4 p.m. Admission is $3 for adults, $2.50 for seniors 62 and above, $2 for students, and free for ages 5 and under.

DINNER Finally, wrap up your Waco weekend by heading back to I-35 for dinner at **George's Waco** (1925 Speight Ave.; 254-753-1421; www.georges restaurant.com), which serves down-home fare and college grub such as wings, chicken tenders, burgers, and Tex-Mex, as well as the signature "Big O" beers. This place is much loved by everyone from Baylor students to famous musicians— there's even a country song called "George's Bar." Open Mon through Sat from 6 a.m. to midnight. Closed Sun.

There's More . . . .

Museum. **Red Men Museum and Library.** Interesting museum dedicated to the Red Men. 4521 Speight Ave.; (254) 756-1221; www .redmen.org.

Recreation. **Jimmy Bryant Horseshoe Complex.** One of the top pitching facilities in the state. Located on the Brazos River in Cameron Park East; (254) 750-5980.

Shopping. **Richland Mall.** Shopping mall featuring dozens of well-known stores. 6001 W. Waco Dr.; (254) 776-6631; www.richland mall.com.

   Spice Village. Fun shopping district with a nice variety of stores. 2nd Street and Franklin Avenue; (254) 757-0921; www .spicewaco.com.

Sports. **Waco Regional Tennis and Fitness Center.** Great place to get a workout and play some tennis. 900 W. Lake Shore Dr.; (254) 753-7675; www.wacotennis.com.

Theater. **Waco Hippodrome Theater.** Performing arts company with a variety of shows open to the public. 724 Austin Ave.; (254) 752-9797; www.wacoperformingarts.org.

Special Events & Festivals . . . .

APRIL
Brazos Nights, Waco. Monthly free concerts held at the Suspension Bridge starting in Apr and ending in July; www.brazosnightswaco .com.

Cotton Palace Pageant, Waco. Annual stage event that tells the story of Waco. Held at Waco Hall at Baylor University; www.waco cottonpalace.org.

AUGUST
Margarita & Salsa Festival, Waco. Heat up, then cool down with this event, held at the Heart of Texas Fair Complex. (254) 776-1660; www.hotfair.com.

SEPTEMBER
Waco Cultural Arts Fest, Waco. This event aims to celebrate cultural differences through the arts. www.wacoartsfest.org.

West Fest, West. Annual polka festival held in the nearby town of West. www.westfest.com.

OCTOBER
Heart O' Texas Fair and Rodeo, Waco. Annual rodeo featuring bronc riding, calf scrambling, funnel cakes, and more. www.hotfair.com /hotfair.

Other Recommended Restaurants & Lodgings . . . . .

Bed and Breakfast on White Rock, 267 Ruby Dell Lane; (254) 799-9783; www.whiterockcreek.com. Serene B&B in a lovely setting.

Clay Pot, 920 I-35 south; (254) 756-2721. Delicious Vietnamese fare located just off the highway.

Courtyard Waco, 101 Washington Ave.; (254) 752-8686; www .marriott.com. Centrally located hotel with easy access to the Waco Convention Center.

Cricket's Grill and Drafthouse, 221 Mary Ave.; (254) 754-4677; www.cricketsgrill.com. A local favorite for pool and drinks.

Dock's Riverfront, 100 I-35 north; (254) 714-2993. Great dinner, drinks, and view.

Hilton Waco, 113 South University Parks Dr.; (254) 754-8484; www.hilton.com. Located downtown, this hotel is convenient to most local attractions.

Judge Baylor House B&B, 908 Speight Ave.; (888) 522-9567; www .judgebaylorhouse.com. Quaint, charming B&B with full breakfast.

La Familia, 1111 La Salle Ave.; (254) 754-1115. Solid Tex-Mex cuisine.

For More Information . . . .

City of Waco; www.waco-texas.com.

Waco Convention and Visitors Bureau; (800) 321-9226; www .wacocvb.com.

Waco Tribune; www.wacotrib.com.

NORTHBOUND ESCAPE *Four*
Fort Worth
CULTURE AND COWBOYS IN FORT WORTH / 1 NIGHT

> Cowboy culture
> Fort Worth Stockyards
> Museums
> Great restaurants

With its location just thirty-five minutes from the heart of Dallas, it would be easy to initially dismiss a weekend trip to Fort Worth. After all, what could Fort Worth possibly offer that Dallas doesn't already have?

As it turns out, quite a lot. From its beginnings as a cattle town to its current reign as a hotbed for culture and art, this multifaceted city will impress you with its lust for life. Saddle up, my friends—it's time to take a ride.

DAY 1/MORNING

Hop on I-45 north and set your cruise control—you're going to be here for about 200 miles. Then, merge onto US 287 north and get ready for a pit stop.

BREAKFAST Most famous for its monstrous DeLuxe fruitcake, **Collin Street Bakery** (at I-45 and US 287 from exit 229; 903-872-2157; www.collinstreet .com) also features a host of breakfast offerings sure to satisfy those early-morning hankerings. Grab a gourmet coffee and a scone, muffin, or Danish and have a seat in the dining room, where plantation-style architecture will transport your far from the highway—for a few minutes. The bakery opens Mon through Sat at 7 a.m. and Sun at 11 a.m. Call for more information.

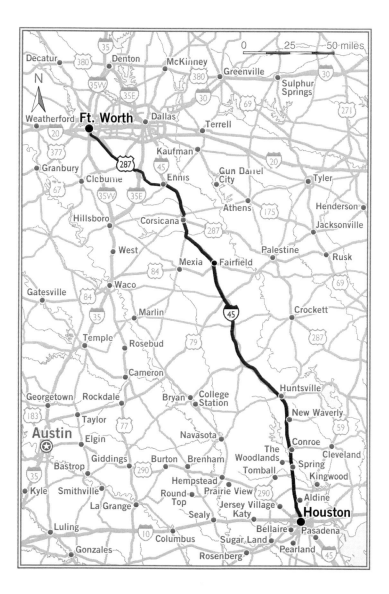

After breakfast, take US 287 to I-30 west and exit at University Drive (exit 12A) to the **Fort Worth Botanical Gardens** (3220 Botanic Garden Blvd.; 817-871-7686; www.fwbg.org), which offer a self-proclaimed "sanctuary for the senses." Located in the city's Cultural District, this place couldn't be more inviting, from its incredible rose garden that will make you feel as if you're part of the Tournament of Roses to the utter peace you'll find on a bench in the Four Seasons garden. Traveling with kids? Be sure to stop by the Japanese Garden to feed the koi fish that beg for food pellets at the surface of the water.

More a fan of feathered friends and felines? Take a right on University Drive and a left on Colonial Parkway until you reach the **Fort Worth Zoo** (1989 Colonial Parkway; 817-871-7050; www.fort worthzoo.com). While it may not be as well-polished as some of the state's other offerings, this zoo—which happens to be the oldest in the state—is a wonderful way to spend part of a morning. Kids will love the interactive exhibits and up-close access to the animals, and parents will enjoy the price: $12 for adults, $9 for kids ages 3–12 and seniors, and free for children under 3. Open 365 days a year.

From the zoo, walk across Colonial Parkway until you see the Forest Park Depot, where you can buy tickets for the **Forest Park Miniature Railroad** (817-336-3328; www.fpmt.us). Built in the late 1950s, the train runs in a 5-mile, forty-minute loop around Forest and Trinity Parks. In addition to being a pleasant way to get a general feel for the area, it's also fun to see the various bridges (including a 350-foot girder bridge and a 171-foot truss bridge) you pass along the way.

LUNCH   Take University Drive north to N. Main Street and go left, then turn right on N. 22nd Street. Turn left on N. Commerce Street and stop at **Joe T. Garcia's** (2201 North Commerce St.; 817-626-4356; www.joets.com) for lunch and a cocktail on the lush garden patio. The homemade tortillas, chiles rellenos, and chimichangas are among my favorites. Need a souvenir? Take home a bottle of their homemade salsa.

AFTERNOON

After lunch, drive north a block, take a right on Exchange Avenue, and park. You're now officially in the **Fort Worth Stockyards National Historic District** (East Exchange Avenue; 817-624-4741; www.fortworthstockyards.org), where you'll want to stay for the remainder of the day.

For a nice introduction to Cowtown, start at the **Stockyards Museum** (131 E. Exchange Ave., Suite 113; 817-625-5087; www .stockyardsmuseum.org), which chronicles the history of the city, which began as a major livestock shipping point and later played host to world's first indoor rodeo. Open daily except Sun; a $2 donation is recommended.

Next, mosey on down to the **Cowtown Cattlepen Maze** (145 E. Exchange Ave.; 817-624-6666; www.cowtowncattlepenmaze .com), 5,400 square feet of twists and turns that will confuse even your smartest human. Compete against the clock for prizes, or laugh at your friends from the raised observation deck. Admission is $5.

A trip to the Old West wouldn't be complete without a cattle drive, and you're in luck—**The Fort Worth Herd Cattle Drive** (East Exchange Avenue; 817-336-4373; www.fortworthstockyards.org) takes place at 11:30 a.m. and 4 p.m. daily along East Exchange Avenue. You'll get a kick out of watching two or three cowboys try to keep their herd of more than a dozen on track.

DINNER　　By now you're certain to have worked up an appetite, so walk up to Main Street and turn left. At **Cattlemen's Steak House** (2458 N. Main;

817-624-3945; www.cattlemenssteakhouse.com), you can enjoy lobster, sides, and every type of meat you can imagine. If you want, you can even pick out your own steak and tell the cook how to prepare it.

NIGHTLIFE Always wanted to ride a mechanical bull? Here's your chance. Every Fri and Sat night **Billy Bob's Texas** (2520 Rodeo Plaza; 817-624-7117; www.billybobstexas.com) hosts a live bull-riding competition. Not into that sort of thing? This famous dance hall has plenty of other options, from live music to a "photo bull" to line dancing.

Need a nightcap? Round the corner back to Exchange Avenue, where the **White Elephant Saloon** (106 E. Exchange Ave.; 817-624-8273; www.whiteelephantsaloon .com) awaits with strong shots, upbeat live music, a divey decor, and a very friendly staff.

LODGING The motto at the **Stockyards Hotel** (109 E. Exchange; 800-423-8471; www.stockyardshotel.com), located up the street and around the corner from Billy Bob's, is "Old West at its best," and that certainly seems to ring true. From the cowhide decor in the rooms to the saddle bar stools in the downstairs Booger Red's Saloon, you'll feel right at home on the range.

DAY 2/MORNING

BREAKFAST Take E. Exchange Avenue to N. Main Street, then go right on W. Northside Drive, which will turn into University Avenue, where you'll find one of my all-time favorite Fort Worth experiences: brunch at **Blue Mesa** (1600 S. University; 817-332-6372; www.bluemesagrill.com). From big-as-your-plate waffles to incredible Adobe Pie (peppers, chicken, corn, and masa) to made-to-order omelets, this is one of the best feasts you can find. Even better? The $17.95 price also includes beverages such as unlimited mimosas and poinsettias (cranberry juice instead of orange juice). Service starts at 9 a.m.

From breakfast, go north on University to Darnell Street and park at the **Modern Art Museum of Fort Worth** (3200 Darnell; 817-738-9215; www.themodern.org). This gorgeous building includes floor-to-ceiling windows, and the artwork inside isn't bad, either. Featuring 3,000 pieces by artists such as Pablo Picasso, Jackson Pollock, Susan Rothenberg, and Andy Warhol, this museum is a great way to kick off your trip to the Museum District. Admission is free the first Sun of every month and every Wed.

Next, go west on Darnell, left on Rip Johnson Drive, right on W. Lancaster Avenue, and left on Gendy Street to reach the **Fort Worth Museum of Science and History** (1600 Gendy St.; 817-255-9300; www.fwmuseum.org), a newly renovated building filled with fun and interesting exhibits. Did you know that Texas has more than 430 native species of butterflies (more than any other state)? Or that the pigment and markings of eggs are created by glands in the female bird's uterus and oviduct and are applied onto the egg as it passes through the reproductive system? Once you visit the museum, you will.

Then head next door to the **National Cowgirl Museum and Hall of Fame** (1720 Gendy; 800-476-3263; www.cowgirl.net), which is dedicated to "preserving and teaching the history of the American cowgirl." Think historic rodeo gear, interactive chuck wagon displays, costumes worn by Hollywood starlets, and even a bucking bronco. Admission is $8 for adults and $7 for seniors and children 3–12.

LUNCH Done with the museum district? Go south on Gendy Street to Harley Avenue and go right. Then take a right onto Montgomery Street, go right on Camp Bowie Boulevard and then left on Summit Avenue (becomes W. Weatherford). Turn right on Houston Street and park near **Reata** (310 Houston St.; 817-336-1009; www.reata.net), a favorite Creole and Southern-inspired eatery in Sundance Square. A cocktail on the rooftop patio is particularly wonderful in good weather.

AFTERNOON

You're now in the heart of **Sundance Square** (817-255-5700; www .sundancesquare.com), a 35-block entertainment district that features restaurants, bars, clubs, shops, nightlife, and restored buildings.

One of the most interesting aspects of the square is **Bass Performance Hall** (4th and Calhoun Streets; 817-212-4325; www .basshall.com), a beautifully built structure that has been named one of the top ten opera houses in the world. Whether you go to see the orchestra, the opera, the ballet, the celebrated Van Cliburn International Piano Competition, or simply to tour the facility, you'll appreciate this magnificent place. Public and private tours are available; call to make arrangements.

Finally, stroll down Main Street to the **Ashton Hotel** (610 Main St.; 866-327-4866; www.theashtonhotel.com) for a fantastic afternoon tea at the **Six 10 Grille**. Held Thurs through Sat from 2 to 4 p.m., this English-style event includes your choice of nearly a dozen teas, champagne, soup, empanadas, tea sandwiches, scones, tarts, and madelines. Make reservations twenty-four hours in advance.

From here, you've got about a four-hour drive ahead of you, so it's time to hit the road.

There's More . . . .

Museum. Kimbell Art Museum. Small but impressive art collection. 3333 Camp Bowie Blvd.; (817) 332-8451; www.kimbellart.org.

Nature. **Fort Worth Nature Center and Refuge.** Urban wilderness with 25 miles of hiking trails. 9601 Fossil Ridge Rd.; (817) 392-7410; www.fwnaturecenter.org.

Fort Worth Water Gardens. Relaxing park with three pools. 1502 Commerce St.; (817) 871-5757; www.fortworth.com.

Sports. **Fort Worth Cats.** Professional baseball team. 301 Northeast 6th St.; (817) 226-2287; www.fwcats.com.

Texas Motor Speedway. NASCAR and Indy Car racing. 3545 Lone Star Circle; (817) 215-8500; www.texasmotorspeedway.com.

Special Events & Festivals . . . .

JANUARY

Fort Worth Stock Show and Rodeo. Three weeks of high-energy rodeo events. (817) 877-2400; www.fwssr.com.

APRIL

Main Street Arts Festival. An annual free arts event held on Main Street between the Tarrant County Courthouse and the Fort Worth Convention Center. (817) 336-2787; www.mainstreetartsfest.org.

MAY

Mayfest. Four days of family-friendly entertainment, live music, and crafts in Trinity Park. (817) 332-1055; www.mayfest.org.

OCTOBER

Fort Worth Alliance Air Show. Flight displays, interactive booths, and more at the Fort Worth Alliance Airport. www.allianceairshow.com.

Other Recommended Restaurants & Lodgings . . . . .

The Ashton Hotel, 610 Main St.; (817) 332-0100; www.theashton hotel.com. Historic yet modern hotel in downtown Fort Worth.

Courtyard Downtown/Blackstone, 601 Main St.; (817) 885-8700; www.marriott.com. Lovely yet affordable Marriott near Sundance Square. Rates from about $130.

Etta's Place, 200 W. 3rd St.; (817) 255-5760; www.ettas-place .com. Charming bed-and-breakfast in the heart of everything.

Love Shack, 110 E. Exchange Ave.; (817) 740-8812; www.shake yourloveshack.com. Hamburger joint in the Stockyards.

Omni Fort Worth, 1300 Houston St.; (817) 535-6664; www.omni hotels.com. Luxury meets hospitality at this hotel, located near the convention center.

Paris Coffee Shop, 704 West Magnolia Ave.; (817) 335-2041; www .pariscoffeeshop.net. Gritty, unassuming, sure-to-please breakfast and lunch spot.

Pour House, 2725 W. 7th St.; (817) 335-2575; www.pour-house .com. Great Sundance Square bar with delicious pub grub.

Railhead BBQ, 2900 Montgomery St.; (800) 978-3211; www.rail headonline.com. Widely regarded as the best meats in town.

Riscky's BBQ, 300 Main St.; (817) 877-3306; www.risckys.com. Delicious barbecue since 1927.

For More Information . . . .

The Dallas/Fort Worth Area Tourism Council; http://dfwandbeyond .com.

Fort Worth Chamber of Commerce; www.fortworthcoc.org.

Fort Worth Convention and Visitors Bureau; (800) 433-5747; www .fortworth.com.

NORTHBOUND ESCAPE *Five*

Dallas
BIG FUN IN BIG D / 2 NIGHTS

Culture and the arts

Great food

Vibrant nightlife

Six Flags Over Texas

First-rate shopping

Outside of Texas, Dallas may be known for three things: big hair, big personalities, and a little family named the Ewings. Heck, even the Dallas Convention and Visitors Bureau slogan is "Live large, think big."

To informed Texans, however, Dallas is known as a cultural and commercial hub, with some of the best museums, shopping, and food in the state.

Sure, there's traffic, and yes, big hair, but if you look a little below the surface, you'll find plenty to keep your schedule packed for a weekend trip. Between the sports teams, concerts, bars, and attractions, you may just find yourself going back again and again. Haven't been before? Here's a solid, comprehensive itinerary to get you started.

DAY 1/MORNING

To get to Dallas, simply take I-45 north until you reach the Dallas–Fort Worth metro area.

BREAKFAST   From I-45 north, take the Main Street West/Elm Street exit (exit 284B) to Pacific Avenue and go right. Turn right on N. Malcolm X Boulevard and right on Elm Street until you reach **Café Brazil** (2815 Elm St.; 214-747-2730; www .cafebrazil.com). One of several locations in the DFW area, this beloved coffee shop/ cafe serves some of the best breakfast fare in Dallas. Signature menu items include

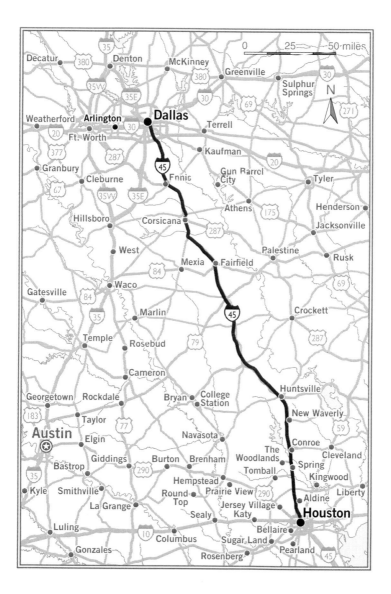

pulled chicken tacos, smoked turkey migas, chilaquiles, and a breakfast relleno filled with scrambled eggs, chorizo, and cheddar, as well as a full coffee bar. And don't miss the fantastic rosemary potatoes. Open 7 a.m. to midnight Sun through Thurs and twenty-four hours on Fri and Sat.

Next, go west on Elm Street until you reach the **Sixth Floor Museum at Dealey Plaza** (411 Elm St.; 214-747-6660; www.jfk.org), a fantastic museum that gives you access to the spot where Lee Harvey Oswald is believed to have shot John F. Kennedy in 1963. Within the museum, you can view films, photographs, and artifacts from the time leading up to and following the assassination, as well as take an audio tour of the building. Don't miss the incredible sniper's perch and the staircase where Oswald is believed to have escaped: both have been preserved to look exactly as they did in 1963.

Then, go east on Elm Street to N. Houston Street and take a left, then take a right on Ross Avenue. From there go left on N. Griffin Street and end at the **Dallas World Aquarium** (1801 N. Griffin; 214-720-2224; www.dwazoo.com), where creatures from five continents are waiting to greet you. Expect exhibits on South Africa, the rain forest and Borneo, as well as animal talks, feedings, and performances. Don't miss the gentle manatees as they cruise through the water or the majestic jaguar as it examines its surroundings. Open daily from 9 a.m. to 5 p.m. Admission is $20.95 for adults, $16.95 for seniors 60 and older, $12.95 for children 3–12, and free for children 2 and under.

Next, go northwest on N. Griffin Street to Corbin Street and go left, then turn left on N. Lamar Street/TX 354 Loop. Go right onto Elm Street/TX 354 Loop south, then right on N. Market Street, and stop at the **West End Marketplace** (along Market and Record Streets near downtown; 214-741-7180; www.dallaswestend.org). This historic district located right next to downtown is filled with attractions, shops, and restaurants. Highlights include the **Dallas**

Holocaust Museum (211 N. Record St.; 214-741-7500; www
.dallasholocaustmuseum.org), **Dallas Segway Tours** (1907 N.
Lamar St. in the lobby of Springhill Suites Hotel; 972-821-9054;
www.dallassegwaytours.com), and **House of Blues Dallas** (2200 N.
Lamar St.; 214-978-2583; www.houseofblues.com).

Done checking it out? From the West End, go south on N.
Record Street to Elm Street/TX 354 Loop south and turn right.
Then go left on N. Houston Street/TX 354 Loop south and left
on Main Street until you reach **Pegasus Plaza** (1500 Main St.;
www.pegasusnews.com). This $2.5 million park/plaza is a popu-
lar meeting spot for Dallas residents because of its ample shade,
winding stream, and relaxing fountains. While you're there, stop in
the **flagship Neiman Marcus** (1618 Main St.; 214-741-6911; www
.neimanmarcus.com), which opened in the early 1900s and features restaurants, a salon, a fifth-floor museum, and several floors
of cutting-edge fashion.

LUNCH Since you're at Neiman's already, go by **Zodiac** (inside Neiman Marcus, 1618 Main St., on level six; 214-573-5800; www.neimanmarcus.com),
a historic upscale restaurant serving up standard fare such as sandwiches and
salads, as well as famous items such as popovers and mandarin orange soufflé.
Open 11 a.m. to 3 p.m. Mon through Sat. Closed Sun.

AFTERNOON

Now it's time to get your culture on in the outstanding Dallas Arts
District. Start by going west on Main Street to N. Field Street,
heading right, and then taking a right onto Woodall Rodgers Freeway. Take that to N. Harwood Street and go right to end at the
Dallas Museum of Art (1717 N. Harwood; 214-922-1200; www
.dm-art.org). This world-class museum features 24,000 works of

art inside a beautiful 370,000-square-foot building designed by Edward Larrabee Barnes. The exhibits, which cover 7,000 years, include ancient Americas, Africa, Indonesia, and Southeast Asia; European and American painting, sculpture, and decorative arts; and American and international contemporary art. Plan to spend several hours here. Open 11 a.m. to 5 p.m. Tues and Wed, 11 a.m. to 9 p.m. Thurs, and 11 a.m. to 5 p.m. Fri through Sun. Special events are held throughout the week; check the website for details and admission fees.

From there, walk northwest on Harwood Street and turn right on Flora Street to the **Trammell and Margaret Crow Collection of Asian Art** (2010 Flora St.; 214-979-6430; www.crowcollection .com). This impressive collection includes a permanent set of galleries dedicated to China, Japan, India, and Southeast Asia and features pieces from as early as 3500 BC to as late as the early twentieth century. Open since 1998, the museum was created with the mission of informing the general public about artists from these areas and their work. Open from 10 a.m. to 9 p.m. Tues through Thurs and 10 a.m. to 6 p.m. Fri through Sun. Closed Mon. Admission is free.

Then, head down the street to the **Nasher Sculpture Center** (2001 Flora St.; 214-242-5100; www.nashersculpturecenter.org), a fantastic indoor-outdoor museum featuring interesting, unexpected work from artists such as Henri Matisse, Pablo Picasso, Joan Miró, and Alberto Giacometti. Browse the indoor galleries using an audio tour, then reflect in the perfectly designed outdoor garden. Open 11 a.m. to 5 p.m. Tues through Sun. Closed Mon. Check the website for admission details.

DINNER By now you've probably worked up an appetite, so head northeast on Flora Street to Olive Street and go left, then turn right on Woodall Rodgers Freeway. Merge onto US 75 and take exit 2 toward Knox Street/Henderson

Avenue. Go right on N. Henderson Avenue and end at **Victor Tangos** (3001 N. Henderson Ave.; 214-252-8595; www.victortangos.com). This sexy spot features "urban bar fare" and a variety of drinks, such as craftsman brews, made-from-scratch cocktails, and quality wines. Happy hour is all day Mon and 5 to 7 p.m. Tues through Fri. In terms of the food, the menu is made up primarily of large and small bites, with options such as ahi tuna nachos, homemade lamb sausage with oven-dried tomatoes and manchego, lobster BLT sliders, warm duck confit salad, jerk spiced prawns with papaya and plantains, and chicken and waffles. Don't miss the spectacular hanger steak and flatbread. Opens at 5 p.m. Mon through Sat; closed Sun.

NIGHTLIFE   Looking for a nightcap? Go southeast to N. Henderson Avenue until you see Willis Avenue and go right. Then, turn right on N. Central Expressway/US 75 north and U-turn to US 75 south. Go right on N. Fitzhugh Avenue, left on Cole Avenue, left on Lemmon Avenue, and left on McKinney Avenue until you reach **The Loon** (3531 McKinney Ave.; 214-559-3059), known for extremely strong drinks and occasionally celebrity clientele (Owen Wilson has been known to hang out here). Just limit yourself to one or two cocktails—otherwise chances are good you'll be needing a cab to get home.

LODGING   For can't-miss lodgings that are convenient to most Dallas attractions, book a room at the **Stoneleigh Hotel and Spa** (2927 Maple Ave.; 800-921-8498; www.stoneleighhotel.com). This luxury boutique hotel is located in Dallas's Uptown District and features a hip 1920s art deco design, a full-service spa, a sleek restaurant and bar, and upscale guest rooms with luxury linens, flat-screen HD TVs, huge windows, high-speed Internet access, and more.

DAY 2/MORNING

BREAKFAST   Start your day at Stoneleigh's **Bolla** restaurant, where breakfast is served daily from 7 a.m. to 10:30 a.m. Menu items include biscuits and sausage gravy; an Uptown omelet with smoked salmon, crème fraîche, and chives;

a Texas Benedict with braised short ribs, chipotle hollandaise, and biscuits; and gingersnap blueberry pancakes.

Next, go southeast on Maple Avenue and take a right on N. Pearl Street, then go right on Woodall Rodgers Freeway to I-35 east and merge onto I-35 ES/US 77 south toward Waco. Merge onto I-30 west (via exit 428D) and exit on Six Flags Drive to **Six Flags Over Texas** (2201 Road to Six Flags St. in Arlington; 817-640-8900; www.sixflags.com). This popular theme park includes all kinds of attractions, shows, and rides, including the breathtaking Mr. Freeze, the jaw-dropping Superman: Tower of Power, and the fun Silver Star carousel. The park also offers a VIP pass that gives visitors automatic access to the front of ride lines and special seating at shows. Once you get your fill of rides and pose with a couple of superheroes, cool down with a signature Pink Thing—a sherbet concoction that's a park favorite. Check the website for hours, admission, and discounts.

Want a different kind of amusement? Head to **TopGolf** (8787 Park Lane; 214-341-9600; www.topgolf.com), an amazing golf entertainment complex that features a full-size driving range with ball tracking and instant personalized feedback about your swing and game. Open to players of all levels; golf club rental is free. The complex also includes a full-service restaurant, bar and lounges, meeting space, corporate and event facilities, patios, a TopGolf Academy, a TopGolf Junior Academy, minigolf, and batting cages.

After you've had your entertainment, go get your greens at the **Dallas Farmers Market** (1010 S. Pearl Expressway; 214-939-2808; www.dallasfarmersmarket.org). One of the largest public farmers' markets in the country, this complex features a variety of fresh local produce, from watermelons to avocados to tomatoes. Pick up all the fresh produce you can handle at Shed 1, then head over to Shed 2, where vendors offer specialty food such as coffee, cheese, meats, and pastries. The market also offers cooking classes on Sat and hosts special events throughout the year. Open daily from 8 a.m. to 6 p.m.

LUNCH Hungry yet? From the market, go right on Cadiz Street, left onto S. Central Expressway, left onto N. Pearl Street, right at McKinney, and left at Fairmount Street to **Nick and Sam's Grill** (2816 Fairmount St.; 214-303-1880; www .nick-samsgrill.com), a casual bistro featuring traditional American comfort food. Most menu items here, which range from teriyaki chicken drummettes to a grown-up grilled cheese to roasted chicken with Yukon gold mashed potatoes, are under $20. Call for hours.

AFTERNOON

Next, head to **Victory Park** (located at the intersection of I-35, N. Dallas Tollway, and the Woodall Rodgers Freeway; www.victorypark .com), a multiuse dining-shopping-entertainment complex that links various areas of Dallas. While the park itself is worth a visit, a major draw is the eight "super screens"—four on each side of the main plaza—that broadcast everything from works of art to Dallas Mavericks games. Rather watch basketball in person? Head to the adjacent American Airlines Center to see the **Dallas Mavericks** (2500 Victory Ave.; 214-665-4797; www.nba.com/mavericks). Check the website for schedule and ticket prices.

From the center, take I-30 east/US 67 north until you reach the 2nd Avenue exit toward Fair Park. Go right on 2nd, then left on Ash Lane, then left on 1st Avenue/TX 352. From there, turn right on Commerce Street and stop for happy hour at the **Double Wide** (3510 Commerce St.; 214-887-6510), a popular bar/music venue in the hip Deep Ellum area. Expect kitschy decor, great music, and affordable cocktails. Call for hours and cover charge.

DINNER While you're in the area, stop for dinner at the **Twisted Root Burger Co.** (2615 Commerce St.; 214-741-7668; www.twistedrootburgerco.com). This joint serves up a variety of burgers—regular, cheddar, buffalo, venison, turkey, and veggie—as well as salads, shakes, and fries. Don't miss the delicious blue cheese and jalapeño burger with a side of fried green beans. Open 11 a.m. to 9 p.m. Sun through Thurs and 11 a.m. to 10 p.m. Fri and Sat.

DAY 3/MORNING

BREAKFAST Before you head home, start your day at **Highland Park Pharmacy** (3229 Knox St.; 214-521-2126), a fantastic little soda shop/restaurant with a wonderful breakfast selection that remains both charming and cheap. Lunch is also a solid bet: Think grilled cheeses and lime freezes. Open at 7 a.m. Mon through Sat and 10 a.m. Sun.

There's More . . . .

Culture. **African American Museum.** Home to a variety of exhibits including one of the largest African-American folk art collections in the country. 3536 Grand Ave.; (214) 565-9026; www.aamdallas .org.

Entertainment. **Whirly Ball.** Fun, challenging mix of lacrosse, basketball, and bumper cars. 3641 W. Northwest Hwy.; (214) 350-0117; www.whirlyball.info.

History. **Dallas Firefighters Museum.** Interesting museum with a collection of antique fire equipment such as a horse-drawn steam pumper and early model motorized engines. Great for kids. 3801 Parry Ave.; (214) 821-1500; www.dallasfiremuseum.com.

Frontiers of Flight Museum. Cool exhibits covering the history of flight and the role Dallas played in it. 6911 Lemmon Ave.; (214) 350-3600; www.flightmuseum.com.

The Women's Museum. More than 70,000 square feet honoring the contributions of women over history. 3800 Parry Ave.; (214) 915-0860; www.thewomensmuseum.org.

Outdoors. **White Rock Lake Park.** City-operated lake and park offers a hike-and-bike trail, bird-watching, picnic areas, and more. 8300 E. Lawther Dr.; (214) 670-8740; www.dallasparks.org.

Shopping. **Dallas Galleria.** Huge shopping center stocked with a range of stores, an ice rink, a playplace, and restaurants. 13350 Dallas Parkway; (972) 702-7100; www.galleriadallas.com.

View. **Dallas Arboretum and Botanical Garden.** Lovely, peaceful place to spend an afternoon. 8525 Garland Rd.; (214) 515-6500; www.dallasarboretum.org.

Special Events & Festivals . . . .

FEBRUARY
AutoRama, at Dallas Market Hall, 2200 Stemmons Freeway; (248) 373-1700; www.autorama.com. Major touring custom car show.

MARCH
Dallas Blooms, at the Dallas Arboretum, 8525 Garland Rd.; (214) 515-6500; www.dallasarboretum.org/special_events/blooms.html. The largest floral festival in the South, with more than 500,000 spring-blooming bulbs.

Savor Dallas, at various venues; (888) 728-6747; www.savordallas
.com. Fabulous wine and food festival with more than sixty-five
chefs and a bunch of beverages including wines, spirits, and beers.

APRIL
Deep Ellum Arts Festival, in the historic Deep Ellum neighborhood;
(800) 538-1881; www.meifestivals.com. A weekend-long celebration of art, music, and creativity.

JULY
Taste of Dallas, at Fair Park; www.tasteofdallas.org. Three-day
event featuring the best chefs and restaurants, as well as nationally
known bands.

SEPTEMER
Greek Food Festival of Dallas, call for location details; (972) 233-
4880; www.greekfestivalofdallas.com. Celebrate Greek dancing,
food, shopping, and culture at this annual event.

Other Recommended Restaurants & Lodgings . . . . .

Café Pacific, 24 Highland Park Village; (214) 526-1170; www
.cafepacificdallas.com. Upscale seafood spot in the Highland Park
area.

Five Sixty, 300 Reunion Blvd. E.; (214) 741-5560; www.wolfgang
puck.com. A Wolfgang Puck project located in Reunion Tower with
fabulous views of the city.

Good 2 Go Taco, 702 N. Buckner Blvd.; (214) 668-0831. Affordable taco joint in the Lakewood area.

Hotel Adolphus, 1321 Commerce St.; (214) 742-8200; www.hotel adolphus.com. In Dallas since 1912, this hotel has a long and storied tradition of high-class service.

Hotel Lawrence, 302 S. Houston St.; (214) 761-9090; www.hotel lawrencedallas.com. Affordable hotel near many major attractions.

Hotel ZaZa, 2332 Leonard St.; (214) 468-8399; www.preferred hotels.com. Sexy hotel perfect for an upscale getaway. Try booking during the week for really low rates.

Magnolia Hotel, 1401 Commerce St.; (214) 915-6500, www.mag noliahoteldallas.com. Boutique hotel in the heart of downtown.

Mansion on Turtle Creek, 3411 Gillespie St.; (214) 559-2100; www.mansiononturtlecreek.com. Upscale hotel known for its incredible restaurant.

Medieval Times, 2021 N. Stemmons Freeway; (866) 731-9313; www.medievaltimes.com. A fun night out for dinner and a medieval-themed show.

Purple Cow, multiple locations; www.bitwerkz.com/purplecow. Family-friendly spot with fun fare.

Taco Bueno, multiple locations; www.tacobueno.com. Popular fast-food taco chain perfect for a late-night snack.

Teppo Yakitori and Sushi Bar, 2014 Greenville Ave.; (214) 826-8989. Delicious sushi and Japanese cuisine.

Wingfield's Breakfast and Burgers, 2615 S. Beckley Ave.; (214) 943-5214. Favorite brunch and burger spot located in south Dallas.

For More Information . . . .

Dallas Convention and Visitors Bureau; www.visitdallas.com.

Dallas County; www.dallascounty.org.

General Dallas information; www.dallas.com.

SOUTHBOUND ESCAPES

SOUTHBOUND ESCAPE *One*
Rockport-Fulton
AN ARTISTIC, AND HISTORIC, ADVENTURE / 2 NIGHTS

Birding
Art galleries
Seafood
Beach activities
Laid-back vibe

Nestled next to some of the cornerstones of Texas history and located in a county comprising primarily peninsulas, islands, and bays, it's no wonder that Rockport-Fulton's diverse makeup makes it home to a bevy of attractions. The local bays, which include Aransas Bay, Copano Bay, Mesquite Bay, St. Charles Bay, and Port Bay, to name a few, attract a multitude of wildlife including whooping cranes. On top of that, it's a popular artists' community that makes for lots of unique shopping and souvenir opportunities. Whether you're craving a weekend in the wilderness or time in an artistic enclave filled with boutiques, galleries, and museums, you'll find it here.

DAY 1/MORNING

From Houston, take US 59 south toward Victoria, then take US 77 south to TX 239 and go left. Go right onto TX 239/TX 35 and follow TX 35 to TX 35 BR south. Go straight onto Broadway Street/TX 70, follow that to E. Market Street, and go right and you'll be in Rockport.

BREAKFAST When you get about twenty minutes outside Houston on US 59, exit on W. Airport Boulevard and go to **59 Diner** (12550 S.W. Freeway; 281-242-5900; www.59diner.com), part of a Houston chain that serves up some of the best

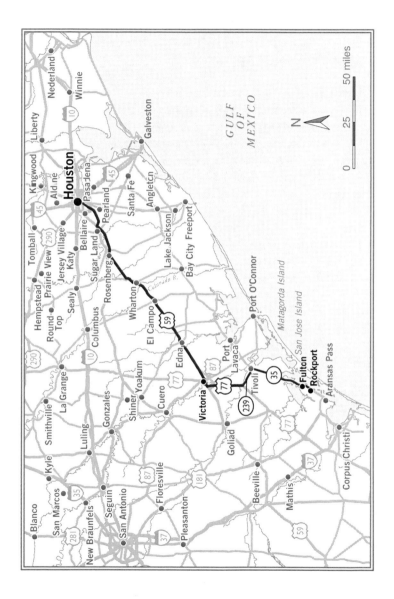

breakfasts around twenty-four hours a day. Favorite dishes include breakfast tacos, omelets, migas, and pancakes. And don't miss the cinnamon roll, which is made from scratch and will set you back just $2.99.

LODGING After breakfast follow exit signs to BR 59 and go left until you reach the **Tee Pee Motel** (4098 E. US 59 BR in Wharton; 979-282-8474; www .teepeemotel.net), where each room is shaped like an individual tepee. Sound bizarre? It is, but in a fun way. The rooms are spacious, clean, comfortable, and affordable. Plus, you can tell all of your friends you've stayed in a real tepee, which is priceless. Each of the ten rooms has a private bath, refrigerator, microwave, and hair dryer. No two rooms are alike; free Wi-Fi is available in each. There is also an RV park available on-site. Call for details.

Next, get back on US 59 south and stay on it until you see the exit for TX 111, then go right on TX 111 until you see signs for **Lake Texana State Park** (46 Park Road 1 in Edna; 361-782-5718; www .tpwd.state.tx.us). This lovely 575-acre park features a sparkling lake with 125 miles of shoreline. Popular activities include camping, boating, Jet Skiing, waterskiing, sailing, canoeing, swimming, birding, and fishing. Don't miss the interpretive programs offered on Sat in the summer and year-round by appointment.

Now, take TX 111 back to US 59 and go south until you see the US 59 BR south ramp toward Telferner/Victoria and take that. From there, go left onto N. Moody Street/US 59 BR, then right on W. Stayton Avenue, then left onto Memorial Drive to the **Texas Zoo** (110 Memorial Dr. in Victoria; 361-573-7681; www.texaszoo.org), which calls itself the "little zoo with the big heart." Located inside of Riverside Park, the zoo comprises primarily animals native to Texas, such as armadillos, river otters, prairie dogs, snakes, alligators, and more. It is also home to endangered species such as the red wolf, ocelot, bald eagle, and jaguarundi. Open daily from 9 a.m. to 5 p.m. General admission is $5 for adults, with discounts for children, seniors, and members of the military. Special events are also held throughout the year; call ahead for details.

LUNCH Now go southeast on Memorial Drive and take a right on W. Stayton Avenue, then right on N. Moody Street/US 59 BR. Turn left at Goodwin Avenue and right on Main Street and stop at the **Rosebud Fountain and Grill** (102 S. Main St. in Victoria; 361-573-5111; www.rosebudfountain.com), a 1940s-era soda fountain and restaurant serving up delicious, home-cooked meals. Menu items include everything from burgers and onion rings to salads and sandwiches to frog legs and catfish. Open Mon through Sat from 11 a.m. to 2:30 p.m. and Fri and Sat from 5:30 to 9 p.m.

That not strike your fancy? Instead, try **Toscana Artisan Bakery and Bistro** (6322 N. Navarro; 361-579-9597), which serves a variety of food centered around its wood-fired oven. Open Tues through Sat for breakfast, lunch, and dinner.

AFTERNOON

Now that you're well fed, set out down US 59 south for a Texas history tour. From US 59 south, go left on S. Jefferson Street/US 183, turn right on Park Road 6/TX P6A and go until you see **Goliad State Park** (108 Park Road 6; 361-645-3405; www.tpwd.state.tx .us). Anyone familiar with Texas history will recognize the stories about this area—and Presidio La Bahia specifically. It's the place where Col. James W. Fannin and his men were held before being executed by order of Santa Anna. The park also contains the Zaragoza Birthplace State Historic Site, the Fannin Memorial Monument, and Mission Espíritu Santo State Historic Site. Even if you're not a history buff, a visit to this place is a sobering and interesting experience. You can even make reservations to stay overnight in the priest's quarters. While you're there, be sure to stop by **La Bahia Gift Shop** (38 Camino De Bexar; 361-645-3939), which is stuffed with random, entertaining artifacts including an authentic cannonball.

After you're done touring, cool off at the **Goliad Paddling Trail** (361-645-3405; www.tpwd.state.tx.us), a 6.6-mile river trail that follows the San Antonio River with access points within the park. Fishing and bird-watching are among the activities available on the trail. Admission is $3 for each person 13 or older.

Next, go east on US 59 until you see the exit for FM 2987/ Fannin, then turn south onto FM 2506 and end at the **Fannin Battleground State Historic Site** (734 FM 2506 in Fannin; 512-463-7948; www.visitfanninbattleground.com), where Colonel Fannin and his men surrendered during the Battle of Coleto Creek. You can walk the grounds of the historic two-day battle, view a monument dedicated to Fannin, or check out an interpretive exhibit.

Let's move from battles to houses with our next site, the **Fulton Mansion State Historic Site** (317 Fulton Beach Rd. in Rockport; 361-729-0386; www.visitfultonmansion.com). To get there, take US 59 south to US 77 south and go right, then take the ramp to TX 239/TX 35 and follow TX 35 to TX 35 BR. From TX 35 BR, go left on Henderson Street, then right on S. Fulton Beach Road, where you'll see the mansion. From the outside, the 1877 mansion is a beauty, surrounded by oak trees and located right next to Aransas Bay. The inside is equally impressive, from its elaborate gardens to its gas lighting to its flushing toilets. Guided tours are mandatory and begin on the hour Tues through Sat from 10 a.m. to 3 p.m. and Sun from 1 to 3 p.m. Call ahead for availability. Admission is $6 for adults, $4 for ages 6–18, and free for children 5 and under.

DINNER You're at the coast, so it's time to get a heaping helping of seafood up the street at the **Boiling Pot** (201 S. Fulton Beach Rd. in Rockport; 361-729-6972; www.theboilingpotonline.com), a local institution that serves up some of the best crab, shrimp, sausage, potatoes, and corn around. That all sound delicious? Then order the Cajun combo, which includes all of those items perfectly seasoned and dumped in a huge pile on your butcher-paper-covered table. The Cajun combo is a must-do at the Boiling Pot, but if you're not very hungry, they also serve items such as gumbo, red beans and rice, king crab legs, crawfish, oysters, and boudin. Open Mon through Thurs from 4 to 10 p.m., Fri and Sat from 11 a.m. to 11 p.m., and Sun from 11 a.m. to 10 p.m.

Want another option? Try **Paradise Key Island Grill** (39 Mazatlan, Key Allegro in Rockport; 361-727-0000; www.paradisekeyislandgrill.com), which is located at the Marina on Key Allegro and affords gorgeous sunset views. The menu is a mix of seafood, steaks, and pub grub, and the cocktails can't be beat.

LODGING If you chose not to book a tepee room after breakfast, here are a few more options to consider. For a beautiful, relaxing stay, don't miss the **Lighthouse Inn at Aransas Bay** (200 S. Fulton Beach Rd. in Rockport; 866-790-8439; www.lighthousetexas.com), a seventy-eight-room boutique hotel with outdoor grills and large rooms, many with private balconies. Call ahead for rates.

For a funkier option, try **Fulton Beach Bungalows** (130 Prairie Rd. at N. Fulton Beach Road in Rockport; 361-790-9108; www.fultonbeach.com), which offers colorful private bungalows located right next to the water. Rooms have antique and vintage furnishings, barbecue pits, full kitchens, screened porches, and more. Maid service, however, is not provided.

DAY 2/MORNING

BREAKFAST One way to start your day is at the **Lighthouse Inn at Aransas Bay** (200 S. Fulton Beach Rd. in Rockport; 866-790-8439), which offers a full complimentary continental breakfast with coffee, juice, and pastries to all guests.

Want something different? Swing by **Alice Faye's Restaurant and Bar** (910 N. Fulton Beach Rd.; 361-729-6708), a casual, affordable breakfast spot located right on the bay. The breakfast menu includes eggs, grits, omelets, pancakes, taquitos, and more. Opens daily at 7 a.m. Closed Tues.

Now, go north on S. Fulton Beach Road and turn left on Palmetto Avenue to find **Goose Island State Park** (202 Palmetto St.; 361-729-2858; www.tpwd.state.tx.us), which is located on Aransas Bay and offers plentiful birding, fishing, and boating options. Guided nature hikes are available year-round; birding hikes are Jan through Apr. If you like to camp, the park also offers beachfront camping with amazing views of the bay. Day-use admission is $5 a person for those 13 and up.

While you're at the park, you can't miss **The Big Tree,** a state champion coastal live oak thought to be more than 1,000 years old (according to the Texas Forest Service). It is also one of the largest of its kind in the nation, with a circumference of more than 35 feet, a crown spread of 90 feet, and a height of about 45 feet. As you stand under its branches, which seem to stretch toward the sky like gnarled fingers on an ancient hand, you can't help but wish the tree could share some of the stories it has seen.

Then, follow TX 35 north to FM 774 and go right, then turn right on FM 2040 until you see the gate for **Aransas National Wildlife Refuge** (off FM 2040 near San Antonio Bay; 361-286-3559; www.fws.gov/southwest/REFUGES/texas/aransas). Originally established as a breeding ground for migratory birds, the refuge now includes more than 115,000 acres. It is best known for being home to the largest wild flock of endangered whooping cranes, which roosts on-site every winter. From Nov through Mar, sightseeing boats give visitors a different sort of view of the cranes. Other favorite wildlife includes javelina, roseate spoonbill, armadillo, and white-tailed deer. Open daily from 8:30 a.m. to 4:30 p.m. Admission is $3 a person or $5 for two or more people in a vehicle. And if you're in the park during whooping crane season (Oct–Mar), don't miss watching the birds feed from the observation deck during daylight hours.

LUNCH For lunch, head back to Fulton Beach Road and stop at **Cheryl's By the Bay** (112 S. Fulton Beach Rd.; 361-790-9626; www.cherylsbythe bay.com), which serves fresh comfort fare with a multicultural edge. Menu items include whole poached artichoke in butter with green chile mayo, grilled pork steak and mango quesadilla, fried oyster salad, shrimp coconut curry, fish-and-chips, and Brazilian-style black beans and rice with grilled pork. Art lover? Don't miss the "bodacious burrito for Jackson Pollock." Open for dinner on Mon and Thurs through Sat and open for brunch on Sun from 11 a.m. to 2 p.m. Closed Wed and Thurs.

AFTERNOON

Now, spend some time getting to know the Rockport-Fulton area. Start by getting to know your local artists at the **Rockport Center for the Arts** (902 Navigation Circle in Rockport; 361-729-5519; www .rockportartcenter.com), which spotlights some of the best area, regional, and national artists around with more than one hundred pieces of art in three galleries. There is also a Garden Gallery in the back with a 10,000-square-foot sculpture garden. Admission is free. Open Tues through Sat from 10 a.m. to 4 p.m. and Sun from 1 to 4 p.m. Closed Mon.

Since Rockport-Fulton is home to more than 300 artists—it has been known as an art colony since the late 1800s—it's only appropriate to spend some time exploring its more than fifteen art galleries with coastal, wildlife, contemporary abstract, and Texas Modernist pieces. Stop by the Chamber Visitor Center for a brochure listing locations and hours, or simply take a stroll down Austin Street, where most of them are located. Some recommended galleries include **Austin Street Gallery** (501 S. Austin St.; 361-790-7782), **Coastal Creations Art Gallery** (415 S. Austin St.; 361-790-8101), **Salt Flats Gallery & Photography Studio** (415 S. Austin

St., #9; 361-288-2752), and **Simon Michael Art Gallery** (510 E. King St.; 361-729-6233).

While you're on Austin Street, don't forget to do some shopping. Rockport has a variety of shops, from antiques to furniture to souvenirs. If you're shopping with the girls, drop by **Sassy** (416 S. Austin; 361-790-5030), an adorable boutique with jewelry, trinkets, paintings, cute wine toppers, baby gifts, and more. Prefer to make your own jewelry? Stop by **Jack and the Bead Stock** (115 N. Austin St.; 361-729-1155), where you can select from hundreds of beads and then make your own accessories in a jewelry class.

DINNER For a true taste of Rockport, enjoy dinner at **Latitude 2802 Restaurant & Art Gallery** (105 N. Austin St.; 361-727-9009; www.latitude2802 .com), which offers fresh, upscale dining in an affordable, creative atmosphere that includes an on-site gallery. Menu items include escargot, salmon with capers, medallions of duck, and blackened chicken. And don't miss dessert, which includes crème brûlée, cheesecake with amaretto sauce, and Sambuca chocolate mousse with fresh berries. Opens Tues through Sun at 5 p.m. Closed Mon.

DAY 3/MORNING

BREAKFAST/LUNCH Recharge after your fun night of art and food by heading north on S. Fulton Beach Road, turning right on Henderson Street, left on TX 35 BR south, and left on Magnolia Street to the **Apple Dumpling Deli** (114 N. Magnolia; 361-790-8433; www.rockportdelirestaurant.com). Featuring salads, soups, and fresh apple dumplings, this little restaurant is the perfect place to fuel up for your drive home. Don't miss the French dip, served on freshly baked bread with au jus on the side.

There's More . . . .

Beach. **Rockport Beach Park.** Lovely beach perfect for swimming, fishing, picnicking, and boating. 210 Seabreeze Dr.; (361) 729-8560; www.cityofrockport.com.

Nature. **Aquarium at Rockport Harbor.** Small aquarium featuring Texas plants and animals. 702 Navigation Circle; (361) 729-2328; www.rockportaquarium.com.

Museums. **Market House Museum.** This building, which was first used in 1853, became a firehouse in 1886 and a museum in 1967. Located at Franklin and Market Streets in Goliad; (361) 645-8767.

Texas Maritime Museum. Details Texas maritime history, from settlement to shipbuilding to searching for offshore oil and gas. 1202 Navigation Circle; (866) 729-2469; www.texasmaritime museum.org.

Recreation. **Rockport Aquatic and Skate Park.** Swimming pool, children's pool, nature trail, and skate park available year-round. 2001 Stadium Dr.; (361) 729-2213; www.cityofrockport.com.

Special Events & Festivals . . . .

JANUARY
Gospel Music Festival, a three-day celebration of gospel music; www.gospelforce.org/festival.html.

MARCH
Fulton Oysterfest, held on the Fulton waterfront; (361) 463-9955; www.fultontexas.org. A salute to everyone's favorite bivalve with carnivals, live music, vendors, games, and an oyster-eating contest.

MAY
Rockport Festival of Wines, at the Texas Maritime Museum, 1202 Navigation Circle; (866) 729-2469; www.texasfestivalofwines.com. A weekend of wine-related events, tastings, and cooking demos.

JULY
Rockport Art Festival, at the festival grounds next to the art center; (361) 729-5519; www.rockportartcenter.com. More than 120 artists come together to celebrate art, sell their creations, and enjoy live music, food, and art, of course.

SEPTEMBER
Hummer/Bird Celebration; www.rockporthummingbird.com. A celebration of ruby-throated hummingbirds that includes speakers and refreshments.

Other Recommended Restaurants & Lodgings . . . . .

Arandas Mexican Grill, 2841 TX 35 north; (361) 727-9151; www .arandasmexicangrill.com. Solid Tex-Mex with a varied menu.

Bellino's, 523 S. Fulton Beach Rd.; (361) 729-9003; www.bellino rockport.com. Cozy Italian joint with authentic cuisine.

Capt. Benny's Seafood, 103 S. Fulton Beach Rd.; (361) 729-2013. Delicious seafood with marvelous views.

FaiFoo Café, 1231 W. Market St.; (361) 727-0278. Solid Vietnamese food with good service.

Hemingway's Bar & Grill, 1008 E. North St.; (361) 729-7555; www.hemingwaysbarandgrill.com. Upscale restaurant with incredible steaks and seafood.

Jama's Kitchen, 415 S. Austin St.; (361) 729-5007. Breakfast and lunch joint famous for its cheesecake.

Laguna Reef, 1021 Water St.; (361) 729-1742; www.lagunareef .com. Relaxing waterfront condos and suites.

For More Information . . . .

City of Rockport; www.cityofrockport.com.

General Rockport information; www.rockportnet.com.

Rockport-Fulton Chamber of Commerce; www.rockport-fulton.org.

SOUTHBOUND ESCAPE *Two*

Port Aransas

AN ODE TO THE OCEAN, TEXAS STYLE / 2 NIGHTS

Beach activities

Great seafood

Deep-sea fishing

Dive bars

Funky shops

Everyone has his or her favorite little beach town.

My parents started taking us to Port Aransas for weekend trips when we were kids, and since then it has become a beloved getaway for the whole family. We'll drive down on a Friday night—it takes about three and a half hours to get there—and stay at a rented condo or beach house. Then we'll spend the days frolicking in the ocean, shopping in town, or fishing on the jetty and spend the nights eating scrumptious seafood, checking out local bands at dive bars, or simply looking up at the blanket of stars. The beauty of this beach town is that it's still small—the population remains less than 10,000—but there's enough to do to keep you from getting bored over a weekend. It's one of my favorite places in Texas, and I have a feeling it will be one of yours as well.

DAY 1/MORNING

From Houston, take US 59 south toward Victoria to US 77 south and then go left onto TX 239. Next, go right onto TX 239/TX 35 and follow that to FM 3036/TX 35. Go left onto TX 35 south and merge onto TX 35 south/TX 35 Bypass. Go left on TX 188, right on TX 35 BR south, then left on TX 361. Follow that to the TX 361 ferry. Once you cross, you're in Port Aransas.

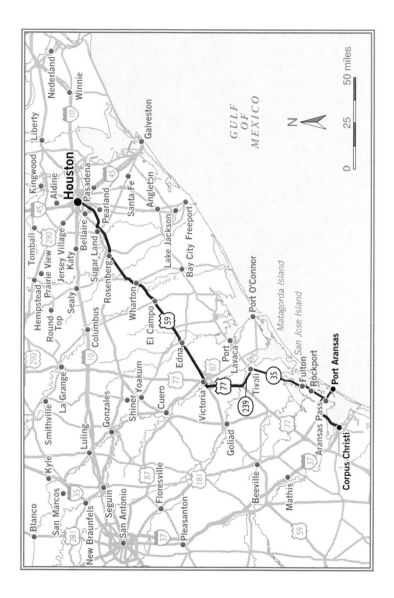

BREAKFAST   Once you get about 30 miles out of Houston, exit on 1st Street in Rosenberg and go right on Avenue H to **Bob's Taco Station** (1901 Avenue H; 281-232-8555; www.bobstacos.com), a fantastic little local institution that claims to have some of the best breakfast tacos in the county. I'll take it further—these are some of the best in the state. Sure, the recent feature by Guy Fieri on Food Network's *Diners, Drive-Ins, and Dives* has brought more crowds to the restaurant, which features homey decor and cute signs with sayings like, "Taco to you later," but the food is worth any wait you might have. Don't miss the melt-in-your-mouth carne guisada tacos, which double as a bargain at $1.95. Opens weekdays at 6 a.m. and weekends at 7 a.m.

While you're in Rosenberg, stop 2 blocks over at the **Rosenberg Railroad Museum** (1921 Avenue F; 281-633-2846; www.rosenberg rrmuseum.org). This cool little museum was modeled after an original depot and includes features such as a 4,000-piece model train set, Tower 17—the last interlocking tower in Texas—and an 1879 business car.

Once you cross on the ferry, turn right on Beach Street and take it to, well, the beach, for a **sandcastle building lesson** (361-290-0414; http://sandrum.com). Once a year, Port Aransas hosts **Texas Sandfest,** a weekend-long sand-sculpting festival that includes more than 200 sculptors, but visitors can learn year-round thanks to Mark Landrum, aka the Port A Sandcastle Guy. During a sixty- to ninety-minute lesson, Landrum will teach you the basics of digging, stacking, and carving and guide you through the process of creating a gorgeous castle. Call for details.

Since you're already at the beach, drive or walk north toward the **Port Aransas South Jetty** (located on the northeastern tip of the island), a popular fishing spot that allows visitors to walk out across the Gulf of Mexico. On any given day you're likely to see fishermen pulling up trout, mackerel, drum, and shark. Just be careful walking along the pier—the surface is uneven.

Once you've viewed a few catches, walk or drive south down the beach to the Horace Caldwell Pier and catch the **Port Aransas Trolley** (361-749-4111; www.cityofportaransas.org/Transportation .cfm), which runs throughout town and costs only a quarter. Popular stops along the route include the J. P. Luby fishing pier, the Leona Belle Turnbull Birding Center, and the University of Texas Marine Science Institute. The trolley runs daily from 10 a.m. to 6 p.m.

LUNCH Get hungry during your tour? Just hop off the trolley on Alister Street and stop at the **Port Aransas Brewing Company** (429 N. Alister St.; 361-749-2739; www.portabrewing.com). Featuring classic pub grub such as nachos, burgers, and fried cheese sticks as well as nearly a dozen craft beers, this laid-back joint is a good place to grab a bite. Don't miss the tasty Port Aransas Pop Pilsner or the loaded sampler platter, featuring fried shrimp, onion rings, crab-stuffed jalapeño poppers, and more. The pizza is also recommended.

AFTERNOON

Next, go north on Alister to E. Cotter Avenue and go right, then take a left on Tarpon Street and end at the Jetty Boat at Fisherman's Wharf (900 N. Tarpon; 361-749-5448; www.jettyboat.net) for a trip over to **St. Jo Island,** a gorgeous, isolated 28-mile strip that offers wonderful fishing, wildlife-spotting, and swimming opportunities. Whether you take a picnic, go after the big catch, or walk along the shore waiting for shells and sand dollars to wash up, you'll enjoy this isolated little island. And keep your eyes peeled when you're on the Jetty Boat—it's a great place to spot dolphins. Multiple trips daily; call for times and prices.

Once you're back on the mainland, it's time to take a break from all that sun and do some shopping instead. Start at **Stephanie's Stuff** (710 N. Alister St.; 361-749-4422), an adorable boutique located adjacent to Seafood and Spaghetti Works. Stuffed to the brim with items for women of all ages, this shop is a great place to stop for a souvenir (personalized wineglass, anyone?), an outfit (don't miss the fantastic purses), or something fun for the kids (think giant rubber ducks).

Next, go down the street to **Winton's Island Candy Co.** (600 S. Alister St.; 361-749-4773; www.wintonscandies.com), a fun, cluttered little candy shop with old-school classics, bright-colored hard candies, and rows of fudge. Don't miss the really good "Good," a nutty caramel concoction that's the store's signature dish.

Wrap up your shopping excursion at the **Family Center IGA** (418 S. Alister St.; 361-749-6233; www.familycenteriga.com), a quintessential island grocery store where you can find everything from $1 reading glasses to zodiac mugs to delectable baked goods to a wide variety of beer. The people-watching here, any time of day, is fantastic. Open Sun through Thurs from 6 a.m. to 10 p.m. and Fri and Sat from 6 a.m. to midnight.

DINNER A trip to Port Aransas wouldn't be complete without a visit to **Virginia's on the Bay** (815 Trout; 361-749-4088; www.virginiasportaransas.com), a lovely little restaurant overlooking the water. Go at sunset and sit on the outdoor deck, looking out at the expensive yachts as you sip a margarita. You can't beat it. Menu items include mesquite-smoked yellowfin tuna dip, surf-n-turf, fried shrimp po'boys, and seafood gumbo. Hours vary by season; call for information.

LODGING For ocean views and all the amenities, stay at **Sea Breeze Suites** (407 Beach St.; 361-749-1500; www.seabreezeporta.com), a small hotel/condominium complex located just a short walk from the beach. Each room has a private balcony and kitchen and Wi-Fi, and local calls are complimentary. Stop by the pool after a day at the beach, or hang in your room watching cable. The best part? During the off-season, room rates can be as low as about $65 a night. Rates vary based on season; call ahead for information.

Want something historic? Try the **Tarpon Inn** (200 E. Cotter Ave.; 361-749-5555; www.thetarponinn.com), a quaint bed-and-breakfast that's been around since 1886. The B&B is charming but not for the tech-obsessed; the rooms don't have phones or televisions.

DAY 2/MORNING

BREAKFAST Before a long day at the beach, you need some sustenance, so take a right on Alister to **Island Café and Smokehouse** (301 S. Alister St.; 361-749-6602). This no-frills breakfast joint is a favorite of the locals because it serves up all the classics, such as biscuits and gravy, huevos rancheros, waffles, and taquitos. Don't miss the tender and perfectly sweet pancakes. Call ahead for hours.

Now, hop back on the ferry and take TX 361 to TX 35 west to the **Texas State Aquarium** (2710 N. Shoreline Blvd. in Corpus Christi; 361-881-1200; www.texasstateaquarium.org), a fantastic aquarium where visitors can do everything from dolphin train for a day to see hawks soar above to touch sharks and stingrays. Prices vary by activity; call ahead for hours and prices.

All done at the aquarium? Now go next door to the **USS *Lexington*** (2914 N. Shoreline Blvd.; 361-888-4873; www.usslexington .com), an aircraft carrier commissioned in 1943 that's said to have set more records than any other carrier in U.S. naval history. These days, it's a museum that aims to teach future generations about the ship's important role in U.S. history. You can walk the deck, try out a flight simulator, or even engage in battle at a virtual battle station.

From there, go north on Shoreline Boulevard to Bridgeport Avenue and go left. Then, go right onto W. Causeway Boulevard and take that onto US 181 south. Exit on the left to Bayfront/Shoreline Boulevard and go right at N. Mesquite Street/TX 544 Spur. Then, go left at Coopers Alley and right at Water Street to end at the **Texas Surf Museum** (309 N. Water St.; 361-888-7873; www.texassurfmuseum.com). Dedicated to preserving the history of Texas surfing, this museum features a variety of interesting exhibits such as a collection of classic boards, a mock garage with tools used for shaping a board, a theater that plays surf movies, and a collection of historic photos. Open Mon through Thurs from 10 a.m. to 7 p.m., Fri and Sat from 10 a.m. to 10 p.m., and Sun from 11 a.m. to 5 p.m. Admission is free.

LUNCH Hungry? Head next door to lunch at the **Water Street Oyster Bar** (309 N. Water St.; 361-881-9448; www.waterstreetrestaurants.com), a favorite Corpus Christi restaurant known for delicious soups, salads, and sandwiches as well as a raw bar and sushi menu. Don't miss the WaterStreet roll, a roll made of shrimp, fire-roasted red pepper, and cucumber topped with seared blackened tuna and avocado and finished with poblano cream sauce and jalapeño ponzu.

Or, for something a little different, visit the **flagship Whataburger** (121 N. Shoreline Blvd.), a larger, prettier edition of the hamburger chain located right on the beach. FYI, Corpus Christi is the hometown of Whataburger.

AFTERNOON

Now, it's time to head back to Port Aransas, so hop on I-35 north back to TX 361 and hit the beach for a lesson with **South Coast Kiteboarding** (361-949-3278; www.southcoastkiteboarding.com), which offers surfing and kiteboarding lessons in Port Aransas and Corpus Christi. Kiteboarding as a sport is kind of like a cross between surfing, windsurfing, and parasailing. A variety of lesson packages are available, including kite skills 1.0, a two-and-a-half-hour class that teaches you how to rig, launch, fly, and troubleshoot a kiteboard, as well as basic safety, site orientation, and etiquette. Prices vary by class; call for more information.

Too intense for your blood? Try a **deep-sea fishing adventure** on the *Scat Cat* or *Wharf Cat* at Fisherman's Wharf (900 Tarpon; 361-749-5448; www.wharfcat.com). Trips start at five hours and give you the opportunity to catch anything from red snapper to shark to kingfish. When you get back, let a nearby restaurant cook your catch for you. Prices vary depending on the length of the trip; call ahead for information.

DINNER For dinner, you must visit **Shells Pasta and Seafood** (522 Avenue G; 361-749-7621), which my parents insist is the best restaurant on the island. After going with them, I have to agree. The place is small and the atmosphere is basic, but the food is out of this world. The menu includes a nice variety of pasta, seafood, and appetizers, as well as a host of options offered on the blackboard daily. Don't miss the pepper-crusted tuna or the mussels if they have them when you go—they're both amazing.

NIGHTLIFE In the mood for a nightcap? Go northwest on Avenue G to S. Station Street and go right, then take a right on Beach Avenue to reach **The Gaff** (323 Beach St.; 361-749-5970; www.gotothegaff.com), a lively and surprisingly family-friendly pirate-themed bar featuring cold beer, live music, and good pizza. Ahoy!

DAY 3/MORNING

BREAKFAST On your way out of town, go west on Beach Avenue to N. Station Street and go right, then turn left on E. White Avenue to **Bundy's** (112 E. White St.; 361-749-4826; www.bundysporta.com), a coffee shop/cafe perfect for a morning pick-me-up. Bundy's offers espresso drinks, smoothies, and a variety of baked goods and pastries, as well as breakfast items such as biscuits and gravy and cheesecake-stuffed French toast. Don't miss the delightful (and huge) cinnamon rolls.

There's More . . . .

Birding. **Leona Belle Turnbull Birding Center.** A boardwalk and scope offering views of a variety of wildlife such as birds, alligators, and butterflies. Ross Avenue near the Trolley stop; www.cityofport aransas.org.

Nature. **South Texas Botanical Gardens.** Nine floral exhibits and gardens on 180 acres. 8545 S. Staples St. in Corpus Christi; (361) 852-2100; www.stxbot.org.

Museums. **Selena Museum.** A memorial to Mexican-American singer Selena Quintanilla-Perez. 5410 Leopard St. in Corpus Christi; www .q-productions.com/museum.
   Art Museum of South Texas. Three-story facility designed by Philip Johnson with a nice variety of pieces. 1902 Shoreline Blvd. in Corpus Christi; (361) 825-3500; www.stia.org.

Sports. **Copeland's Dive Center.** Full-service dive shop. 4041 S. Padre Island Dr. in Corpus Christi; (361) 854-1135; www.copelands inc.com.
   Island Watersports. Variety of water sports rentals. 1102 S. Shoreline in Corpus Christi; (361) 537-0789.
   Newport Dunes Golf Course. Scenic Arnold Palmer Signature course located near the water. 265 Palm Island Dr. in Port Aransas; (361) 749-4653; www.newportdunesgolf.com.
   Sky High Adventures. Set up a parasailing excursion here. 136 W. Cotter in Port Aransas; (361) 749-4600.
   Texas Surf Camps. Surf lessons and camps for all skill levels. (361) 749-6956; www.texassurfcamps.com.
   Yachting Center of Corpus Christi. Yachting, sailboard, and kayak rentals. 108 Peoples St.; (361) 881-8503; www.yachtingcc.com.

Shopping. **La Palmera Mall.** Mall with stores including Macy's, Dillard's, Bath & Body Works, Nine West, Lane Bryant, and more. S. Padre Island Dr. at Staples; (361) 991-5718; www.lapalmera.com.

Theater. **Harbor Playhouse.** Community theater that puts on a variety of performances. 1 Bayfront Park in Corpus Christi; (361) 888-7469; www.harborplayhouse.com.

Special Events & Festivals . . . .

MARCH
Corpus Christi Festival of Arts. Three-day celebration of art that includes exhibits, performances, and demonstrations held at the Art Center of Corpus Christi; www.ccfestivalarts.org.

APRIL
Buccaneer Days. Pirate-themed festival featuring music, food, rides, kid zone, outdoor activities, and more. http://bucdays.com.

Texas International Boat Show. Boat races, fishing contests, and exhibitions held at the Corpus Christi Marina. www.txintlboatshow .com.

Texas Sandfest. More than 200 sculptors and 100,000 spectators appreciating the art of sandcastle building. (361) 215-0677; www .texassandfest.com.

OCTOBER
Harvest Moon Regatta. Annual regatta that arrives in Port Aransas and is celebrated with a host of parties. www.harvestmoonregatta .com.

Other Recommended Restaurants & Lodgings . . . . .

CORPUS CHRISTI

Agua Java, 320 Williams St.; (361) 882-0865. Fantastic coffee, pastries, and more.

Crawdaddy's, 414 Starr St.; (361) 883-5432. Variety of food including great seafood.

Knuckleheads, 819 N. Upper Broadway; (361) 882-9997. Barbecue joint with a fun atmosphere.

Omni Bayfront Hotel Corpus Christi, 900 N. Shoreline Blvd.; (361) 887-1600; www.omnihotels.com. Considered the nicest hotel in Corpus Christi, located close to the water.

Radisson Corpus Christi, 3200 E. Surfside Blvd.; (361) 883-9700; www.radisson.com. Well-appointed hotel located next to the beach.

Republic of Texas Bar and Grill, 900 N. Shoreline Blvd. on the twentieth floor of the Omni Bayfront Hotel; (361) 886-3515. High-end steakhouse with a varied menu.

PORT ARANSAS

Coffee Waves Port A, 1007 TX 361; (361) 986-0481. Coffee bar serving espresso drinks, pastries, and free Wi-Fi.

La Playa Mexican Grille, 222 Beach St.; (361) 749-0022. Solid Tex-Mex restaurant convenient to everything.

Liberty Hall, 103 E. Cotter Ave.; (361) 749-1660. Affordable restaurant with a huge selection of burgers.

Sea Shell Village, 502 E. Avenue G in Port Aransas; (361) 749-4294; www.seashellvillage.com. Cute, funky lodging with a laid-back appeal.

Thaiphoon, 315 S. Alister St.; (361) 749-0882. Tasty, affordable Thai food.

Trout Street Bar and Grill, 104 W. Cotter Ave.; (361) 749-7800; www.tsbag.com. Seafood restaurant located near the water.

For More Information . . . .

City of Corpus Christi; www.cctexas.com.

Corpus Christi Chamber of Commerce; www.corpuschristichamber .org.

Corpus Christi Convention and Visitors Bureau; www.visitcorpus christitx.org.

Port Aransas Chamber of Commerce; www.portaransas.org.

EASTBOUND
ESCAPES

EASTBOUND ESCAPE *One*

Galveston

HITTING THE BEACH, TOURING HISTORY, AND TASTING
THE GOOD LIFE IN GALVESTON / 2 NIGHTS

Beach activities

Great seafood

Deep-sea fishing

Dive bars

Funky shops

It's hard to believe than an hour's drive down the highway can transport to you from Houston's concrete jungle to a splendid beach town with enough activities to pack a weekend. But head down I-45 south to Galveston and you'll find just that.

Galveston has had its ups and downs, including natural disasters such as 2008's Hurricane Ike, which ravaged the island, shutting down hundreds of local businesses and displacing thousands of residents. But while some businesses are still recovering, most have rebuilt better than ever, making the Galveston of today a place that must be seen and enjoyed. So block out a weekend, pack some sunscreen, and hit the road: You won't regret a weekend here.

DAY 1/MORNING

BREAKFAST On your way to Galveston, stop off on I-45 south at **Dot Coffee Shop** (7006 Gulf Freeway; 713-644-7669), a twenty-four-hour diner serving up favorites such as the Paris Grand Prix (French toast, eggs, and meat), chicken-fried steak with gravy, sausage omelets, short stacks of pancakes, and strawberry pie. Make sure you ask for rolls when you order (they're delicious) but don't fill up too much, because the portions are enormous.

Rather wait until you get to Galveston to have breakfast? Once you get into town, exit on 61st Street and go 1 mile until you reach Stewart Road. Turn right on

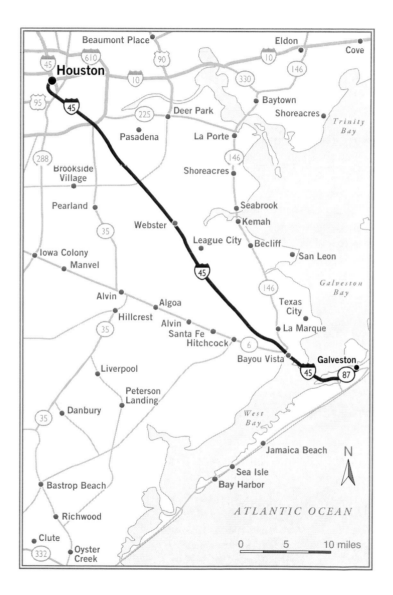

Beaumont Place
Eldon
Cove
Houston
Baytown
Shoreacres
Deer Park
Trinity Bay
Pasadena
La Porte
Brookside Village
Shoreacres
Pearland
Webster
Seabrook
Kemah
League City
Becliff
San Leon
Iowa Colony
Manvel
Galveston Bay
Alvin
Algoa
Texas City
Hillcrest
Alvin
Santa Fe
La Marque
Hitchcock
Liverpool
Bayou Vista
Galveston
Peterson Landing
Danbury
West Bay
Jamaica Beach
N
Bastrop Beach
Sea Isle
Bay Harbor
Richwood
ATLANTIC OCEAN
Clute
Oyster Creek
0   5   10 miles

Stewart Road and go until you reach **Home Cut Donuts** (6807 Stewart Rd.; 409-744-8887), which offers a variety of fresh, homemade doughnuts and kolaches.

Now, go back to 61st Street and turn right, following it until you hit Seawall Boulevard and go left to **Stewart Beach** (201 Seawall Blvd.; www.galveston.com/stewartbeach), one of Galveston's most family-friendly beaches. Sure the water may not be as clear as in the Caribbean and the sand may not glitter as you walk through it, but for a fun-filled escape, you really can't beat it. Rent a beach cruiser from **Island Bicycle Co.** (1808 Seawall Blvd.; 409-762-2453; www.islandbicyclecompany.com) and survey the scene, or pick up a loaf of bread and toss it to the hungry—and friendly—seagulls. The beach includes a children's playground, umbrella and chair rentals, a bathhouse, a souvenir shop, an outdoor pavilion and snack bar, and volleyball courts, as well as special events such as volleyball tournaments and sandcastle competitions in the summer. The park is closed Nov through Feb. Admission is $8.

Next, head south down Seawall Boulevard toward 25th Street until you reach **Galveston Duck Tours** (25th and Seawall; 409-621-4771; www.galvestonducks.com), which will allow you to see the city from an entirely different vantage point. Covering 15 miles, this land and sea adventure gives you up-close access to the Strand shopping district, historic mansions, and the scenery along Offatt's Bayou. Open year-round. Tickets are $15 for adults and $10 for children 2 and up.

After your tour, take a left onto 25th Street and then a right on Harborside Drive to end at **Pier 21,** which is filled with entertainment and dining options. Start at the **Pier 21 Theater** (409-763-8808; www.galveston.com/pier21theatre), which offers regular showings of two movies that detail different historical events of the city. The first, *The Great Storm,* is a twenty-seven-minute documentary about the 1900 hurricane in which 6,000 residents lost their life. The second, *The Pirate Island of Jean Lafitte,* details the life of the famous pirate who spent time on the island.

Next, head next door to the **Texas Seaport Museum** (409-763-1877; www.tsm-elissa.org). The biggest attraction at the museum is the ***Elissa,*** a three-masted, iron-hulled sailing ship built in 1877 that holds the title of "the Official Tall Ship of Texas." Wander across her wooden planks, then head inside the museum, where you'll find special exhibits, educational programs, and a fascinating computer database with the names of more than 130,000 immigrants who made their way to the United States through Galveston.

LUNCH While you're at Pier 21, you might as well take advantage of one of its great restaurants, such as **Fisherman's Wharf** (409-765-5708; www .landrysrestaurants.com), a laid-back seafood restaurant located on the water. Take a seat on the outside deck and enjoy a front-row view of the magnificent tall ship *Elissa,* as well as just-caught tuna, shrimp, and snapper. Don't miss the crab queso or the stuffed shrimp.

AFTERNOON

After lunch, go west on Harborside Drive to 25th Street and turn left. Then, take a right on Seawall Boulevard, then a right on 81st Street, which becomes Hope Boulevard. End at **Moody Gardens** (1 Hope Blvd.; 409-744-4673; www.moodygardens.com). Known for its iconic pyramids, visible from most of Galveston, Moody Gardens is one of the most-loved tourist attractions in the city. And for good reason—the attractions and exhibits here could keep you and your clan busy for at least a full day. Highlights include the penguin encounter program in the Aquarium Pyramid (you get to watch the penguins as they eat, swim, and hang out, from behind the scenes), the multisensory 4D Special FX Theater, the freshwater lagoons and waterfalls at Palm Beach, and the Colonial Paddlewheel Boat.

After Moody Gardens, take a tour of some of Galveston's historical homes by heading back to Jones Road and going right. Then, turn left on Seawall Boulevard, then left on 14th Street and left on Broadway until you reach **Bishop's Palace** (1402 Broadway; 409-762-2475; www.galvestonhistory.org), a gorgeous mansion that was built in 1892 and is noted as one the most "significant Victorian residences in the country." From there, head south on Broadway to the **Moody Mansion** (2618 Broadway; 409-762-7668; www.moodymansion.org), a four-story, 28,000-square-foot home that once belonged to Galveston's influential Moody family.

Continue your tour by heading to **The Strand Historic District,** located along Avenue B between 20th and 25th Streets. This popular district features shops, museums, galleries, bars, and more that are easily accessible to visitors and cruise ship passengers. Start at a unique gift shop called **Hendley Market** (2010 Strand; 409-762-2610; www.hendleymarket.com), which offers fun books, trinkets, and gift items. Then, trek to **La King's Confectionery** (2323 Avenue B; 409-762-6100), a local institution known for its fresh pulled taffy, long candy cases, and huge variety of ice cream flavors, such as pumpkin pie, peanut butter chip, and chocolate chip cookie dough. Next, check out **Karen's Kloset** (2326 Strand St.; 409-539-5429), a fantastic women's boutique with adorable dresses, sexy lingerie, and small gift items. Another favorite boutique is **Jammin' Sportswear** (2314 Strand; 409-763-4005), which is equipped with clothing, souvenirs, and jewelry for all of your beach needs.

DINNER   Getting hungry? Go west on the Strand to 25th Street and turn left. Then, turn right on Seawall Boulevard, then right on 61st Street. End at **Mario's Ristorante** (2202 61st St.; 409-744-2975; www.marios-ristorante.com), an Italian restaurant that has been in Galveston since 1967. The motto here is, "We speak very little English, but we make the best pizza," and if you order one, you can see what they mean. The bacon here is a particular highlight. The portions are gigantic—think soup bowls as big as buckets—and that's a good thing. It's so tasty, you'll want to take all of your leftovers to go.

NIGHTLIFE Continue your evening by heading back to the Strand to catch a performance at **The Grand 1894 Opera House** (2020 Postoffice St.; 800-821-1894; www.thegrand.com), a Galveston landmark listed in the National Register of Historic Places that regularly gets touring acts. Recent visitors have included Smokey Robinson, the B52s, Tuna Does Vegas, and Broadway's Tommy Tune.

Wrap up your night by taking 25th Street back to Seawall Boulevard until you reach **H2o,** the sleek, modern outdoor lounge at the San Luis Resort (5222 Seawall Blvd.; 800-445-0090; www.sanluisresort.com). Next to the pool and spa offering views of the ocean, this bar features expansive seating areas, a fire pit, and high-definition TVs. Drink options range from tropical martinis to upscale wines. Open late on Fri and Sat.

In the mood for something more low key? Visit **Murphy's Pub** (213 22nd St.; 409-762-6177), a great little watering hole with a full bar, cheap beer, a foosball and pool table, and a fantastic jukebox. Not sure if you'll fit in? You will. On any given night, expect to find rugby players, sailors, and celebrity makeup artists (all three were present when I visited). And be sure to tip your bartenders: They're some of the most hardworking IBCs (that's "islanders by choice") you're likely to meet.

LODGING For an upscale experience, stay at the **San Luis Resort** (5222 Seawall Blvd.; 800-445-0090; www.sanluisresort.com), a much-loved, upscale beachfront hotel with a world-class spa, a mouthwatering steakhouse, a sprawling, Vegas-style pool, and a private balcony in each room. Don't miss grabbing a cocktail in the sleek bar, where a band plays Sinatra to tipsy couples who sway starting around 7 p.m. most nights. Room specials and packages are available.

Another option is the **Moody Gardens Hotel** (7 Hope Blvd.; 888-388-8484; www.moodygardenshotel.com), a 242-acre, 100,000-square-foot hotel and convention center located next to Moody Gardens. Room rates can be a little steep, but the views of Galveston and proximity to the gardens make up for it.

DAY 2/MORNING

BREAKFAST Start your day by heading northeast on Seawall Boulevard and turning left on 14th Street to reach **Sunflower Bakery and Café** (512 14th St.; 409-763-5500), which offers a nice variety of breakfast food, brunch, pastries, and sandwiches. Can't-miss items include the bacon and egg sandwich, bread pudding French toast, a shrimp omelet, and filet mignon and eggs. Opens at 7:30 a.m. on weekdays and 8 a.m. on weekends.

Next, spend the morning museum-hopping. Start by going north on 14th Street to Harborside Drive and going left until you reach 25th Street. End at the **Galveston Railroad Museum** (123 25th St.; 409-765-5700; www.galvestonrrmuseum.com). Badly damaged during Hurricane Ike, the museum reopened in summer 2010 and features artifacts from the "golden age of rail travel," including the largest collection of dining ware in the country. The museum also offers model train theaters, three on-site steam engines, scale-model train layouts, and an original Santa Fe Union Station waiting room.

Then, go south on 14th Street until you hit Seawall Boulevard and go right. Follow that until you see 81st Street and turn right, then go left on Cessna Drive. Go right on Beech Street, left on Piper Street, and right on Terminal Drive, where you'll see the **Lone Star Flight Museum** (2002 Terminal Dr.; 409-740-7722; www.lsfm.org) on your right. Home to the Texas Aviation Hall of Fame and a variety of bombers, fighters, and military vehicles, this museum is a great find for any history buffs. Want the experience of actually riding in one of the planes? That can be arranged as well. Call ahead to make plans.

Finally, travel back to Seawall Boulevard and follow that until you reach 51st Street. Go left, until the road becomes Pelican Causeway, and follow that until it dead-ends at **Seawolf Park**

(409-797-5114; www.cavalla.org), home to both the USS *Cavalla* submarine and the USS *Stewart* DE-248 battleship, both of which are open for tours. As you wander through the bedrooms, kitchens, and meeting areas of the gigantic creatures, you can't help but wonder what it would have been like to have been at sea in one for months at a time.

LUNCH Take the causeway to Seawall Boulevard and drive until you reach **Casey's Seafood Café** (3800 Seawall Blvd.; 409-762-9625; www.gaidos .com), a casual restaurant with some of the best seafood on the island. Grab a seat inside, or head to the outdoor picnic tables. Menu items include deep-fried zucchini, a bay shrimp and avocado BLT, lobster tacos, the famous "Juicy Lucy" (a bacon burger covered with chili con queso), Southwest garlic fried chicken, seafood plat- ters, and incredible salads. The bay shrimp salad, Santa Fe crab cake salad, and fajita fish salad are particularly remarkable.

Rather go Greek? Try **Olympia Grill** (4908 Seawall Blvd.; 409-766-1222; www .olympiagrill.net), a family-owned Greek restaurant with a lovely view of the water. Grab an appetizer of feta cheese and olives with pita bread or spinach and pastry spanikopitas, followed by roasted lamb shank, chicken-fried pork chops, or a grilled shrimp pita—you are at the beach, after all.

AFTERNOON

Cross the island to Seawall Boulevard and work off that lunch with a surfing lesson from **Island Surf Camp** (832-279-5560; www .islandsurfcamp.com), which teaches classes to people of all ages and skill levels on the Galveston beach. First, you'll practice how to get up on your board while on shore, then you'll head out to the water to try it firsthand. Instructors Mylinda Carter and Al Clements have been surfing for years and are extremely knowledgeable about Galveston's waves and currents. Lessons start at around $60 an hour.

Next, practice your surfing, sliding, and all other forms of water-related entertainment by heading to **Schlitterbahn Galveston** (2026 Lockheed Rd.; 409-740-3003; www.schlitterbahn.com). Filled with attractions such as the twisting and turning Bahnzai Pipeline body slides, free-falling Cliffhanger speed slides that can sending you flying as fast as 40 miles an hour, and plenty of rides designed specifically for the little ones, you can be sure this park is going to have a little bit of something for everyone.

Finally, round out your day with a round at the **Moody Gardens Golf Course** (1700 Sydnor Lane; 409-683-4653; www.moodygardensgolf.com), a multimillion-dollar, eighteen-hole resort-style public course. A par 72 course designed to be user-friendly, you'll find five sets of tees at each hole to accommodate various abilities.

DINNER Take Seawall Boulevard back to the San Luis Resort for dinner at **The Steakhouse** (5222 Seawall Blvd.; 800-445-0090; www.sanluisresort .com). Expect fine steak, seafood, and wine at this elegantly decorated restaurant that has been ranked one of the best in the state by *Texas Monthly* magazine, the *Galveston County Daily News,* and Tom Horan's Top Ten. Don't miss the escargot, Asian pear salad, or sautéed Gulf snapper with premium lump crab. Traveling as a couple? Try the steakhouse cordial dinner for two, which includes beef tenderloin and grilled shrimp with mashed potatoes and asparagus and a dessert for $95. Swimwear, cutoffs, and jean shorts are not permitted. *TIP:* If the Steakhouse is booked, pull up a seat at the bar, where the full Steakhouse menu is available, as well as a bar menu that includes sushi and perfectly cooked appetizers such as teriyaki chicken and calamari.

NIGHTLIFE For a nightcap, head down Seawall Boulevard toward **The Spot** (3204 Seawall Blvd.; 409-621-5237; www.thespotgalveston.com), a beloved restaurant and tiki bar. Located right next to the ocean and featuring a laid-back yet upbeat open-air vibe, The Spot really is the spot for a burger at lunch, a midday beer, or an after-dinner cocktail. Tiki bar highlights include frozen margaritas and piña coladas (served in a coconut) and an impressive variety of domestic, import, and Texas beers. Call for happy hour specials.

DAY 3/MORNING

BREAKFAST Wrap up your Galveston visit with breakfast at a local institution called the **Mosquito Café** (628 14th St.; 409-763-1010; www.mosquitocafe .com). Fare ranges from a breakfast bowl stuffed with potatoes, fresh spinach, bacon, cheese, and poached eggs to a crustless quiche to a lox and bagel platter. Breakfast is served until 11 a.m., but should you sleep in, their lunch is pretty darn great, as well.

In the mood for brunch? Never fear. The **Sunday Champagne Brunch at the Hotel Galvez** (2024 Seawall Blvd.; 409-765-7721; www.wyndhamhotelgalvez.com) is an island favorite, with a variety of staples including Belgian waffles, pastries, a prime rib carving station, eggs Benedict, and unlimited champagne. Served from 11 a.m. to 2 p.m.

There's More . . . .

Outdoors. Galveston Harbor Tours. Take a fun tour and dolphin watch aboard the *Seagull II,* the Texas Seaport Museum's 50-foot twin-engine boat. Pier 22 at the Texas Seaport Museum; (409) 765-8687; www.galveston.com/harbourtours.

Galveston Island State Park. A beautiful state park that offers day-use and beachside and bayside camping. 14901 FM 3005; (409) 737-1222; www.tpwd.state.tx.us.

Transportation. Galveston Island Trolley. Antique, fixed-rail trolley covers 6 miles including Seawall Boulevard, 25th Street, downtown, the Strand District, the Galveston Wharf, and UTMB Campus. Check the website for a schedule. (409) 797-3900; www.islandtransit.net.

Galveston-Port Bolivar Ferry. Dolphins race, seagulls swoop, and the wind blows through your hair on this free ferry, which is twenty minutes each way. Off TX 87; (409) 795-2230; www.houstontran star.org/ferrywaittimes.

Tour. **Ghost Tours of Galveston.** Visit all of Galveston's best "haunts" with these fun, spooky tours. Call for tours and times. (832) 892-7419; www.ghosttoursofgalvestonisland.com.

Wildlife. **NOAA Fisheries Turtle Hatchery.** Visit rescued baby sea turtles before they make their way back to sea. Call ahead to schedule a tour. (409) 766-3670; http://galveston.ssp.nmfs.gov/seaturtles.

Museum. **Ocean Star Offshore Drilling Rig and Museum.** Experience the life of the offshore drilling industry up-close at a retired jack-up rig. Pier 19 in Galveston; (409) 766-7827; www.oceanstaroec.com.

Special Events & Festivals . . . .

FEBRUARY
Mardi Gras. Galveston loves Mardi Gras, which it celebrates with a two-week festival that includes parades, music, food, galas, and more. www.mardigrasgalveston.com.

OCTOBER
Oktoberfest. This annual event sponsored by First Lutheran Church of Galveston features a weekend of music, German food, beer, auction, raffles, and games. (409) 762-8477; www.firstlutheran galveston.com.

NOVEMBER
Lone Star Bike Rally. A weekend of events that brings together motorcyclists from around the country. www.lonestarrally.com.

DECEMBER

Dickens on the Strand. Hosted by the Galveston Historical Foundation, the popular festival gives visitors a glimpse into life in nineteenth-century Britain. Held in The Strand Historic District; (409) 765-7834; www.galvestonhistory.org.

Moody Gardens Festival of Lights. More than a million lights and a dozen holiday scenes come to life at Moody Gardens. One Hope Blvd., (800) 582-4673, www.moodygardens.com.

Other Recommended Restaurants & Lodgings . . . . .

Benno's on the Beach, 1200 Seawall Blvd.; (409) 762-4621; www.bennosofgalveston.com. Casual, delicious seafood on the seawall.

Best Western, 5914 Seawall Blvd.; (409) 740-1261; www.bestwesterntexas.com. Convenient, affordable lodging located near the ocean.

Commodore on the Beach, 3618 Seawall Blvd.; (800) 231-9921; www.commodoreonthebeach.com. Small, family-friendly hotel (and rates) near the water.

Float, 2828 Seawall Blvd.; (409) 765-7946. Fun patio bar with an on-site pool and views of the ocean.

Gaido's, 3800 Seawall Blvd.; (409) 762-9625; www.gaidosofgalveston.com. Old-school seafood on the seawall.

Hilton Galveston Island Resort, 5400 Seawall Blvd.; (409) 744-5000; www.hilton.com. A comfortable, recently renovated hotel located next to the seawall.

Holiday Inn SunSpree, 1702 Seawall Blvd.; (409) 762-4141; www.ichotelsgroup.com. Nice hotel conveniently located to most Galveston attractions.

Luigi's Ristorante Italiano, 2328 Strand; (409) 763-6500; www .luigisrestaurantgalveston.com. Northern Italian classics in a romantic atmosphere.

The Press Box, 2401 Postoffice St.; (409) 765-5958. Sports bar with great pub grub. Don't miss the bloody Mary.

Saltwater Grill, 2017 Postoffice St.; (409) 762-3474. Elegant, gourmet cuisine located across from the Grand 1894 Opera House. Grab dinner, then head to a show.

Tremont House, 2300 Ships Mechanic Row; (409) 763-0300; www.wyndhamtremonthouse.com. This beautiful, European-style hotel is a local favorite.

Willie G's, 2100 Harborside Dr.; (409) 762-3030; www.williegs .com. Seafood and steaks on the water.

For More Information . . . .

Galveston Chamber of Commerce; www.galvestonchamber.com.

Galveston County website; www.co.galveston.tx.us.

Official website of Galveston Island; www.galveston.com.

EASTBOUND ESCAPE *Two*
Beaumont
A LIVELY TIME OUT EAST / 1 NIGHT

Established in 1838, Beaumont got its start as both a ranching and port town, shipping lumber across the country that was used to rebuild railroads following the Civil War. Its reputation changed forever, though, on January 10, 1901, when the Lucas Gusher on Spindle-

- Boomtown
- Museums
- Shopping
- Gardens
- Swamp activities

top Hill exploded and transformed Beaumont into the home of the first major oil field in the country.

The oil eventually ran out, but Beaumont has since evolved into a town that mixes both old-school charm and new-school fun. And at just an hour and a half outside of Houston, it's the perfect place to go for a quick weekend jaunt.

DAY 1/MORNING

To get to Beaumont, simply get on I-10 east and drive until you see the signs.

ON THE WAY From I-10 east, exit Beltway 8 east (portions toll) and follow that until you cross the Houston Ship Channel. Exit TX 225 east to La Porte, then exit Independence Parkway and go left. Follow the road to the **San Jacinto Monument and Museum** (One Monument Circle in La Porte; 281-479-2421; www.sanjacinto-museum.org). Located at the site of the Battle of San Jacinto, the museum and monument give visitors an educational and entertaining look at the historic fight. The monument, which is the world's tallest memorial column (15 feet taller than the

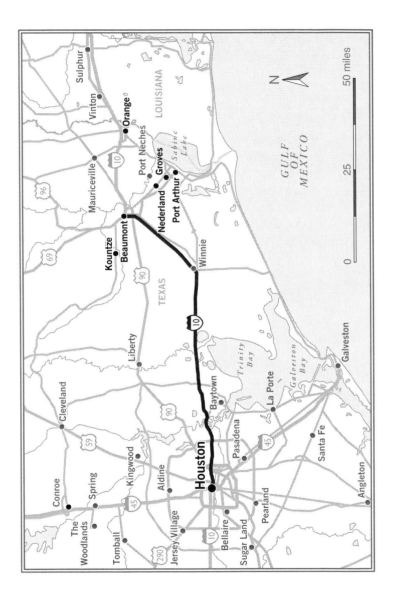

Washington Monument, in fact) offers stunning views from its observation level, and the museum uses art and artifacts to give a fantastic tour of Texas history. Don't miss the adjacent Battleship *Texas,* the last of the battleships patterned after HMS *Dreadnought* to participate in World War I and World War II. Open daily from 9 a.m. to 6 p.m.

BREAKFAST   Once you get near Beaumont on I-10 east, take exit 852B to Calder Avenue and turn right until you reach **Rao's Bakery and Coffee Café** (2596 Calder Ave.; 409-832-4342; www.raosbakery.com). First established in 1941, this quaint little restaurant features items such as pastries, sandwiches, desserts, and gourmet coffee, as well as a full cake menu. Opens Mon through Fri at 6 a.m. and Sat at 7 a.m.

Once you're done with breakfast, go east on Calder Avenue until you reach Main Street and turn right. End at the **Texas Energy Museum** (600 Main St.; 409-833-5100; www.texasenergymuseum .org), which gives visitors a fascinating look at the oil industry, from its beginnings at the Spindletop Gusher to the mechanics of early oil well drilling to the objects it's used to create today. Don't miss all of the interactive exhibits. Admission is $2 for adults, $1 for children 6–12, and $1 for seniors 65 and up. Parking is free. Open Tues through Sat from 9 a.m. to 5 p.m. and Sun from 1 to 5 p.m. Closed Mon.

Next, head next door to the **Art Museum of Southeast Texas** (500 Main St.; 409-832-3432; www.amset.org), which is home to roughly 1,000 pieces of art from the nineteenth, twentieth, and twenty-first centuries with a focus on American and contemporary folk art. Works includes paintings, sculptures, prints, photos, and more. Don't miss John Alexander's *The Beast,* a pastel and charcoal drawing of a crocodile traipsing among the lily pads.

Got your fill of art? Go southeast on Main and take a right on College Street, which becomes US 90 west. From there, go left on the TX 380 Spur, then follow signs to US 69/US 96/US 287 south. Exit at Highland Avenue/Sulphur Drive, then make a U-turn at the underpass. Stop when you see **Spindletop—Gladys City Boomtown Museum** (University Drive and US 287; 409-835-0823; www.spindle top.org). Located the site of the famous Spindletop Gusher, this re-created town lets you see what it was like to live in Beaumont just after oil was discovered. Kids in particular will enjoy wandering through the town's shops and buildings, which include a black-smith shop, a doctor's office, a malt shop, a general store, and a saloon. Don't miss the copy of the early-era *New York Times* that includes a story about the oil discovery. And be sure you take your picture in front of one of the looming wooden oil towers, which stretch up to the sky like miniature Eiffel Towers.

LUNCH   For lunch, get back on US 287 south and follow the ramp to Port Arthur. Follow that until you see the exit for FM 365/Port Neches and take that. Turn left onto FM 365 north, then right onto 9th Avenue until you reach **Dylan's Bar and Grill** (8601 9th Ave.; 409-722-1600; www.dylanson9th.com). When you pull up, don't be intimidated by the windowless, strip-club-like atmosphere—inside is a kid-friendly joint with one of the largest selections of pub grub I've ever seen. Menu items include fried oyster shooters, hush puppies, kitchen sink queso, and several varieties of potato skins, as well as soups, sandwiches, and salads. There's also a full bar—call ahead for daily specials. Open daily from 11 a.m. to 2 a.m.

AFTERNOON

Now, go southeast on 9th Avenue to FM 365 south and go left, then take a left onto US 287/US 69 and follow that until it merges with Woodworth Boulevard. Follow Woodworth Boulevard to Procter Street and go right to end at the **Museum of the Gulf Coast** (700 Procter; 409-982-7000), a 39,000-square-foot museum offering exhibits on everything from the role of Native Americans in the

Gulf Coast region to the impact of the Civil War to tributes to great musicians, sports figures, and actors from the area. One of the most popular areas is the Music Hall of Fame, where a jukebox spins songs by native artists such as Cookie and the Cupcakes, George Jones, and Clay Walker, and a replica of Janis Joplin's intricately painted Cabriolet shines from the corner.

Next, go northeast on Procter Street to TX 87 north and go right. TX 87 north becomes US 90 BR/Green Avenue. From there, go right on N. 5th Street, then right on W. Main Avenue until you see the **W. H. Stark House** (610 W. Main Ave.; 409-883-0871; www .whstarkhouse.org). This immaculate house, which was built at the turn of the twentieth century and features 14,000 square feet with fifteen rooms, is decorated as it was when the Stark family lived there from 1894 to 1936. Original furnishings, silver, glass, artwork, china, and lighting can be seen throughout the house. Tours are available from 10 a.m. to 3 p.m. Tues through Sat. Admission is $5 for adults and $2 for seniors 65 and up and children 10 and up. Children under 10 are not allowed.

Now, it's time to get some fresh air in a beautiful setting. Go west on W. Main Avenue to N. 6th Street and turn right, then go left on US 90 BR/Green Avenue. Go right on N. 16th Street/TX 87, then left on W. Park Avenue to **Shangri La Botanical Gardens and Nature Center** (2111 W. Park Ave.; 409-883-0871; www.shangrilagardens .org). This incredible site was the brainchild of H. J. Lutcher Stark, who wanted to create a haven of "indescribable beauty where time would stand still." He began work in 1937, and in 1946 it opened to the public. Following an ice storm, the park was shut down for more than fifty years, reopening in 2008. Today, the 252-acre garden has attractions that will keep you busy appreciating nature for a full afternoon.

Start your visit with an Outpost Tour, where a guide will take you on a pontoon boat ride through Adams Bayou to a site on the cypress/tupelo swamp. Then, take a guided or self-guided tour of the botanical gardens, where a milelong path will take you past the oranges, purples, and yellows of more than 300 types of plants and wildlife such as butterflies and birds. When you get hungry, stop for a bite to eat at the Star and Cresent Moon Café. Greenhouses, a gift shop, a kid's area, and a nature center are also available on-site. Don't miss the telescopes located throughout the park. I looked in one and was surprised to see that it was set on a group of long-necked white birds that were nesting—a sight I never would have noticed otherwise. Admission price varies depending on tours; hours vary depending on season. Call ahead for details. Closed Mon.

Once you've got your fill of nature, go east on W. Main Avenue to N. 5th Street and turn left. Then, take a right on US 90 BR/Green Avenue and go left on N. Simmons Drive/US 90 BR east. Go left on I-10 west and take that until you reach exit 855A to US 90 west. From there, turn left at US 90 west, then right at Crockett Street and end at the **Crockett Street Entertainment District** (900 block of Crockett; www.crockettstreet.com). This block is filled with dining and nightlife options and has become a hub for locals and visitors looking for a night on the town. Parking is free, and all of the venues are walkable.

DINNER   Start at **Spindletop Steakhouse** (290 Crockett St.; 409-833-2433; www.spindletopsteakhouse.com), an upscale restaurant with an impressive menu. House favorites include a twenty-ounce Tomahawk rib eye, seared ahi tuna, steak bites served with fondue, lumped crab stack, Gulf snapper, and schnitzel. Open for lunch Mon through Fri from 11 a.m. to 3 p.m. and dinner Tues through Thurs from 5 to 10 p.m. and Fri and Sat from 5 to 11 p.m. Closed Sun.

NIGHTLIFE   Next, hit up a few of the bars in the district—there are a variety of options for all tastes. Feel like two-stepping? Head to **Dixie Dance Hall** (234 Crockett St.; 409-833-1881; www.dixiedancehall.com), a dance hall featuring country and popular tunes and occasional concerts from artists like Pat Green, Cross Canadian Ragweed, and Merle Haggard. Not in the mood to country dance? Try **The Hub Lounge and Patio Bar** (260 Crockett St.; 409-833-1881; www.crockett street.com), which combines flat-screen TVs, rock music, ice-cold beer, and a full menu to create a place where you'll want to spend a few hours. Also features live music on weekends. And if you're just in the mood for a good old-fashioned game of pool, try **Star Bar** (296 Crockett St.; 409-813-2299), which features martinis, an outdoor patio, and pool tables, shuffleboard, and video games.

LODGING It may be a chain, but the **Hilton Garden Inn** (3755 I-10; 409-842-5646; www.hilton.com) is affordable, convenient to everything, and very well kept. Don't miss the fresh-baked cookies placed out in the lobby periodically.

DAY 2/MORNING

BREAKFAST Once you're awake, get on I-10 east and take that until you reach US 287 north via exit 853A. Get on that and take the exit to Delaware Street and go left, then turn right on Dowlen Street and end at **Goodfella's** (3350 Dowlen Rd.; 409-861-2500) for Sunday brunch. This classic Italian joint regularly offers some of the best dishes in the area, ranging from bruschetta to Caesar salad to pasta and steak. On Sun, these offerings go into overdrive with food specials and bottomless mimosas. Brunch starts at 10:30 a.m.

Next, spend the afternoon shopping in Old Town's Calder Avenue. Start at the **Calder House Antique Mall** (1905 Calder Ave.; 409-832-3622), which is housed inside an antique home and features a selection of vintage furniture, jewelry, glassware, and collectibles. The owners also pour and sell homemade candles. Then, head to **Granny's Collectibles** (6465 Calder Ave.; 409-892-3210), a packed shop where items such as Madame Alexander dolls and Yankee candles are sure to catch your fancy. Want something for the kids? Check out **Posh Baby** (5955 Phelan Blvd.; 409-860-3331), an adorable store with all kinds of items for your tyke, from organic onesies to room decor to cool rocking chairs.

LUNCH For lunch, go down the street to **Elena's Mexican Restaurant** (6290 Phelan Blvd.; 409-861-2800). A favorite among locals, Elena's serves a variety of Tex-Mex favorites such as fajitas, queso, and tacos. Don't miss the delicious pechuga con queso, in which perfectly cooked, tender chicken breasts are smothered in cheese.

There's More . . . .

BEAUMONT
Museum. **Babe Zaharias Museum.** Nice tribute to sportswoman Babe Didrickson Zaharias. 1750 E. IH-10; (409) 833-4622; www.babedidriksonzaharias.org/museum.cfm.

Outdoors. **Beaumont Botanical Gardens.** Well-maintained garden with walking paths, benches, water amenities, and bird-watching opportunities. 6088 Babe Zaharias Dr.; (409) 842-3135; www.beaumontbotanicalgardens.com.

Adventure. **Cowboy Badlands Extreme Sports Park.** Extreme sports complex featuring motocross, quad racing, and more. 18179 I-10 west in Beaumont; (409) 794-1985; www.cowboybadlands.com.

KOUNTZE
Park. **Big Thicket National Preserve.** Forty miles of hiking trails as well as bird watching, biking, boating, fishing, horseback riding, canoeing, and kayaking are available at this park. 6044 FM 420 in Kountze; (409) 951-6700; www.nps.gov.

NEDERLAND
Museum. **Dutch Windmill Museum.** An interesting three-story tribute to the immigrants from Holland who settled in the town of Nederland. 1500 Boston Ave. in Nederland; (409) 722-0279.

ORANGE
Wildlife. **Super Gator Tours** offers a combination of swamp tours, airboat rides, fishing excursions, and nature studies. 106 E. Lutcher Dr. in Orange; (409) 883 7725.

PORT ARTHUR
Outdoors. **Buu Mon Buddhist Temple.** Gorgeous temple and gardens open to the public. 2701 Procter St. in Port Arthur; (409) 982-9319; www.buumon.org.

Tour. **Texas Marshland Tours** provide access to refuge sites with great birding opportunities. 3262 Bell St. in Port Arthur; (409) 736-3023; www.sabinelakefishing.com.

Special Events & Festivals . . . .

JANUARY
Janis Joplin Birthday Bash, Port Arthur. A celebration of the singer's life organized by the Museum of the Gulf Coast's Music Hall of Fame; www.portarthur.com/janis/index1.html.

MARCH
South Texas State Fair, Beaumont. Carnival, bull rides, rodeo events, food, and more. Held at the Beaumont Fairgrounds; www.ymbl.org/fair.htm.

APRIL

Mauriceville Crawfish Festival, Mauriceville. Popular crawfish festival and cook-off with a pageant, parade, live music, Battle of the Bands, crafts, and more; (409) 651-6358.

Port Neches RiverFest, Port Neches. Celebration of the river featuring boat races, carnival rides, live music, and food. Held at Port Neches Riverfront Park; www.portnecheschamber.com/events.html.

JULY

Orleans Street Jazz Festival, Beaumont. This outdoor festival held in downtown Beaumont features popular local jazz artists and benefits the Southeast Texas Arts Council.

Other Recommended Restaurants & Lodgings . . . . .

BEAUMONT

Best Western Jefferson Inn, 1610 I-10 south in Beaumont; (409) 842-0037; www.bestwestern.com. Friendly, affordable lodging located near I-10.

Courtyard by Marriott, 2275 I-10 south in Beaumont; (409) 840-5750; www.marriott.com. Solid lodging in a comfortable location.

MCM Eleganté Hotel & Conference Center, 2355 I-10 south in Beaumont; (409) 842-3600; www.mcmelegantebeaumont.com. Cool, convenient hotel with all the amenities.

Suga's Deep South Cuisine and Jazz Bar, 461 Bowie St. in Beaumont; (409) 813-1808; www.sugasdeepsouth.com. Southern cuisine with an independent twist.

GROVES
Larry's French Market, 3701 Pure Atlantic Rd. in Groves; (409) 962-3394; www.larrysfrenchmarket.com. Delicious Cajun fare in a down-home atmosphere.

ORANGE
Shangrila Bed & Breakfast, 907 Pine Ave.; (409) 670-1911; www .therogershouse.com. Charming bed-and-breakfast easily accessible from I-10.

PORT ARTHUR
Aurora Bed & Breakfast, 141 Woodworth Blvd. in Port Arthur; (409) 983-4205. Sweet bed-and-breakfast located near the water.

For More Information . . . .

Beaumont Convention and Visitors Bureau; www.beaumontcvb .com.

***Beaumont Enterprise* newspaper;** www.beaumontenterprise.com.

City of Beaumont; www.cityofbeaumont.com.

City of Orange; www.orangetexas.net.

Orange Convention and Visitors Bureau; www.orangetexas.org.

Orange County; www.co.orange.tx.us.

EASTBOUND ESCAPE *Three*

Lake Charles, LA

LOOKING FOR LADY LUCK IN LOUISIANA / 2 NIGHTS

Casinos
Alligators
Wildlife
Airboat rides
Boudin Trail
Cajun food

The fifth-largest city in the state of Louisiana, Lake Charles covers 42.5 miles, bordering Lake Charles and Prien Lake. Settled by various Indian tribes, it was officially incorporated as a city in 1867.

There's always been something about this area that's fascinating to me.

Maybe it's the swamps, with birds, alligators, crabs, and people intermingling like ingredients in a pot of gumbo. Maybe it's the food, from spicy boudin to crawfish to jambalaya. It could be the gaming, with four huge casinos featuring table games, slot machines, and even horse racing within a short distance from one another.

Or maybe it's the whole mix. Whatever it is, southwest Louisiana enchants.

DAY 1/MORNING

To get to Lake Charles, take I-10 east for about two and a half hours until you get to town. Once you get close to Lake Charles, take 1-10 to I-210 east via exit 25 toward Lake Charles Loop. Exit on Nelson Road and turn left, then turn left on Avenue L'Auberge and end at **L'Auberge du Lac Casino** (777 Avenue L'Auberge; 866-580-7444; www.ldlcasino.com). One of four resort casinos in the area, L'Auberge is known for giving visitors an upscale yet comfortable retreat. It's a great place to make your home base for the weekend.

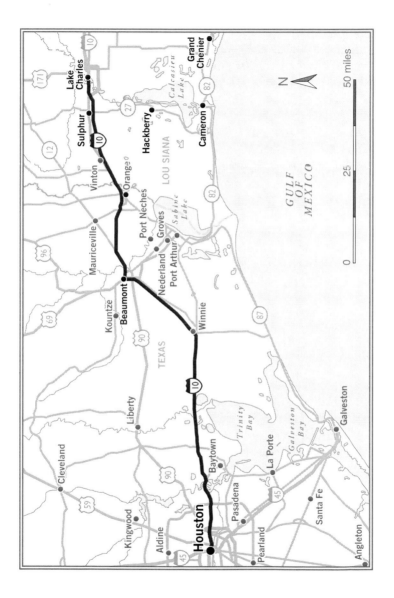

BREAKFAST   You're bound to be hungry, so start at **Le Café** (located on the first floor of the resort), which offers breakfast twenty-four hours a day. Want something quick? Stop by **Lattes** for a cup of joe and a muffin, cinnamon roll, or kolache.

Next, stretch your legs with a round of golf at the on-property **Contraband Bayou Golf Club** (337-395-7220), a Tom Fazio–designed course that incorporates marsh and lowland features to create a fun and unique 7,077-yard, par 71 eighteen-hole course. With eight lakes, four tee boxes per hole, and dedicated beverage cart service, you can be sure you'll have a good time on the green.

Next, cool off with a dip in the hotel's **pool and lazy river,** where fun-seekers of all ages gather to swim, dunk, and be merry. The scene can get a little hectic later in the evening—think college students chugging beer—but early in the morning it's relaxed and comfortable. Kids will love floating on inner tubes around the lazy river pool, and adults will enjoy the swim-up access to frosty beverages from the bar. Poolside cabanas are also available for rent. Pool opens at 10 a.m.

If that's not relaxing enough, head next to the **Spa du Lac** (866-580-7444), an 8,700-square-foot facility that features a variety of treatments, from facials to massages to body treatments. Don't miss the "Wear your cake and eat it, too!" treatment, in which a warm mix of carrots, cinnamon, and vanilla is massaged into your skin and drizzled with warm honey for hydration. Then your skin is exfoliated and moisturized to leave you with a fresh, vitamin-A-heavy glow. Treatments start around $60. The spa is open daily from 9 a.m. to 9 p.m.

Now that you've got your glow on, go test your luck in the **casino,** where 30,000 square feet of gaming, including 60 table games and 1,600 slots, await. L'Auberge is technically the largest single-level riverboat casino in the world, but the hustle and bustle on the floor is more reminiscent of Las Vegas. Open twenty-four hours.

LUNCH Once you've worked up an appetite, it's time to hit the **Southwest Louisiana Boudin Trail** (www.visitlakecharles.org/things-you-must-see5). Pronounced "boo-dan," this local specialty looks like sausage but is filled with a mixture of ingredients such as pork, rice, onions, parsley, liver, and seasonings. Typically it is served as a link or fried into balls. Because of its popularity, the Lake Charles/Southwest Louisiana Convention and Visitors Bureau has created a self-guided trail of the best boudin joints, from restaurants to mom-and-pop markets and grocery stores along I-10 and US 90. Be careful to pace yourself on this tour, however: otherwise you'll be feeling stuffed—and likely sick—by the end of the day.

First, take Avenue L'Auberge to Nelson Road and go right to **Market Basket** (4431 Nelson Rd. in Lake Charles; 337-477-4868). On the outside it may look like a dumpy little grocery story, but inside it's serving up some of Lake Charles's best boudin. Equipped with a smokehouse and a staff that hand-makes the links, Market Basket's boudin has a well-balanced texture and rich flavor. And don't miss their smoked boudin, which offers a unique yet delicious twist on the classic. Call ahead for hours.

Next, go north on Nelson Road to I-210 east and take exit 6A to LA 385/Ryan Street. Go left onto LA 385/Ryan Street, right on E. Prien Lake Road, then left on Kirkman to **Homsi's Tobacco and Beer** (2612 Kirkman St.; 337-439-2323). This place primarily functions as a gas station/liquor store but also sells mild and hot boudin, which is basic but tasty.

From there, go north on Kirkman Street to 17th Street and go right, then go right on Enterprise Boulevard. Next, go right on I-210 west and follow that to I-10 west via the exit on the left. From there, take the LA 1256 exit (exit 20) toward Cameron and go left on LA 27 BR south/LA 1256 to Main Street and end at **Brown's Grocery** (620 Main St. in Hackberry; 337-762-4632). Located in a small grocery store, Brown's offers a mix of items including biscuits, chicken, and boudin. Don't miss the boudin balls for 99 cents each.

AFTERNOON

Tired of boudin? Time to check out another Louisiana staple: swamps. Go south on E. Main Street/LA 27 to Cameron Ferry, then follow LA 27/LA 82 east until you reach **Airboats and Alligators** (1151 Oak Grove Hwy./LA 82 in Gran Chenier; 337-274-2395). Run by area native Ben Welch, the tour gives visitors a comprehensive view of the area marshland, including wildlife such as birds, minnows, and, if you're lucky, alligators. Even if you go at midday, when you're less likely to see any out, Welch will point out interesting spots, such as where an alligator is making her nest or where he last spotted one. It's fascinating stuff, and Welch is a seasoned guide. Just make sure you wear the provided headphones—the boat is loud. Call ahead for prices or to make an appointment.

After your airboat ride, continue down LA 82 to take a tour of the **Creole Nature Trail** (covers 180 miles in southwest Louisiana; 800-456-7592; www.creolenaturetrail.org). This natural corridor offers visitors a glimpse of Louisiana's outback, from its parks and wilderness refuges to its lakes and beaches, including its more than 300 species of birds. Highlights include **Cameron Prairie National Wildlife Refuge,** which is home to wildlife such as deer, geese, ducks, birds, nutria, and alligators and offers interactive exhibits about the area's ecosystem; **Sabine National Wildlife Refuge,** where fishing and crabbing opportunities await at every turn; and the beaches off LA 82 toward **Johnson Bayou,** where candy-colored houses on stilts mingle with the fresh ocean air.

Now, head back to the casino by heading east on LA 82 to LA 27 and going north until LA 27 becomes LA 1256N. Merge onto I-10 east to Lake Charles, then merge onto I-210 east via exit 25 and turn left to Avenue L'Auberge. Once inside, it's time to do a little shopping. Start at **Modele** (337-395-7797), a surprisingly well-stocked women's boutique featuring brands such as BCBC Max Azria, Tommy Bahama, Jessica Simpson, Brighton, and more. Don't miss the excellent sale rack, where you can easily score a pair of peep-toe stilettos for less than $50. Next, visit **Wha'chabringme,** an adorable children's boutique featuring clothes, books, toys, and an array of stuffed animals and dolls for the little one in your life. Looking for something a little more romantic? Try **L'ove,** a lingerie boutique with brands such as Hanky Panky, Cosabella, Belladonna, Spanx, Elle Macpherson, and more, as well as luxury lotions, candles, and bath products.

DINNER Work up an appetite with all that shopping? Head to the **Jack Daniel's Bar and Grill** (337-395-7102), an upbeat restaurant with a noisy yet friendly vibe and a menu featuring all the American classics. Favorites include the ribs, hamburgers, and salads. The restaurant also features a full bar. Opens daily at 4 p.m.

Ready for dessert? Head down the hall to the aptly named **Desserts,** where sweet treats of every type await. Think banana tarts, brownies made with Valrhona chocolate, cheesecake lollipops, more than a dozen types of gelato, and white chocolate macadamia nut cookies, baked fresh every fifteen minutes. Open until 11 p.m. Sun through Thurs and until midnight Fri and Sat.

LODGING With 1,000 hotel rooms, it's easy for travelers of every type to find a room they'll be comfortable with during a day at **L'Auberge**. Basic rooms are about 350 square feet and include a bath/shower combination, warm decor, terry-cloth robes, high-speed Internet, and a flat-screen TV. Suites start at around 550 square feet and include features such as pop-up flat-panel TVs, wet bars, mini-fridges, and oversized claw-foot tubs with separate marble showers. Specials and packages are available.

DAY 2/MORNING

BREAKFAST Grab a quick coffee and pastry at **Lattes** in **L'Auberge.** You've got a big day ahead, so it's time to hit the road.

Go east on Avenue L'Auberge and stay on that to Nelson Road. Head right. Then, merge onto I-210 west, then merge onto I-10 east via exit 1B. Take exit 29 to LA 385/Downtown area and merge onto the N. Lakeshore Drive feeder road. Stop at **the Lake Charles/ Southwest Louisiana Convention & Visitors Bureau and Alligator Pond** (1205 N. Lakeshore Dr.; 337-436-9588; www.visitlake charles.org). First, go inside to pick up information about the town, then head around back to visit the Alligator Pond, a small but ample pond located near the lake's edge. As you peer at the water from behind a wooden barricade, you'll find yourself wondering if that thing you see is an alligator or a log. When it winks at you, you'll know.

Then, follow the feeder road east until you reach Bord du Lac Drive (exit 29) and park near **Veteran's Memorial Park.** Located along the Lake Charles boardwalk, this park pays tribute to all branches of the Armed Forces and is home to a famous WWII Patton Tank. From there, walk south along the boardwalk until you reach **Bord du Lac Park** (900 Lakeshore Dr.; 337-491-1280), where a playground and PPG Interacting Fountain await eager little ones (and little ones at heart).

From there, go south on Lakeshore Drive until you reach Kirby Street and go left. Then take a right on Ryan Street and end at the **1911 Historic City Hall Arts and Cultural Center** (1001 Ryan St.; 337-491-9147; www.cityoflakecharles.com). This former city hall underwent a substantial renovation and in 2004 opened as a public art gallery and cultural facility. Exhibits rotate. Check the website for information. Open 10 a.m. to 5 p.m. Mon through Fri and Sat from 10 a.m. to 2 p.m. A farmers' market is held here on Sat from 8 a.m. to noon.

Go north on Ryan Street to Broad Street and go right to the **Children's Museum** (327 Broad St.; 337-433-9420; www.swlakids .org). This venue offers 19,000 square feet with forty-five hands-on exhibits for the kiddos. Features include a make-and-take art zone, a bubble factory, a kitchen, a rock wall, pulleys, and more. Open Mon through Sat from 10 a.m. to 5 p.m. Admission is $6.50 for adults and children 24 months and up, $5.50 for seniors 55 and up. Free for children 23 months and under.

LUNCH Next, go west on Broad Street to Ryan Street and go left until you reach **Pujo St. Café** (901 Ryan St.; 337-439-2054; www.pujostreet.com). Located inside a beautifully restored building, this cafe/bistro features an extensive menu of seafood and Italian favorites. Don't miss the oysters pujo (pecan-coated oysters topped with spinach, tasso, and smoked Gouda sauce), shrimp bisque, chipotle pepper pasta, or andouille stuffed chicken. Open Mon through Fri from 11 a.m. to 9:30 p.m. and Sat from noon to 9:30 p.m.

AFTERNOON

After lunch, go south on Ryan Street to Kirby Street and go left to the **Mardi Gras Museum of Imperial Calcasieu** (809 Kirby St.; 337-430-0043). Here, you'll find the largest display of Mardi Gras costumes in the world, as well as learn the history of the King Cake and the holiday traditions in southwest Louisiana. You can even climb aboard a parade float. Open Tues through Fri from 1 to 5 p.m. Admission is $3 for adults and $2 for children and seniors.

Now, go next door to the **Black Heritage Gallery** (809 Kirby St., Suite 207; 337-488-0567), where you'll find a variety of exhibits about influential African Americans in the area. Open Mon through Fri from 9 a.m. to 5 p.m.

Then, go west on Kirby to Kirkman Street and turn right, then make a left on Broad Street. Broad Street becomes N. Lakeshore Drive/I-10 Service Drive. Merge onto I-10 west toward Beaumont and take exit 27 toward LA 378, then go left. From there, go left on Sulphur Avenue/LA 378, right on Guillory Street/LA 379, and left on Houston River Road. Next, go right on LA 27, left on E. Harrison Street, and left on Lake Charles Avenue to end at the **DeQuincy Railroad Museum and City Park** (400 Lake Charles Ave. in DeQuincy; 337-786-2823). Located where two major railroads intersected in 1895, this museum features a steam engine, passenger car, and caboose, as well as a library, playground, picnic tables, and pavilion. Open Thurs through Sun from noon to dusk. After that, stroll through town to look for buildings in the historic district, such as All Saints Episcopal Church or the Hagler House.

DINNER   Now, go northwest on Lake Charles Avenue to E. 4th Street and go right, then go right on LA 27 until you reach LA 379. Go left, then take a right on Sampson Street/LA 378. Go right on I-10 east and follow that until you see exit 29 to LA 385. Take a slight right onto LA 385/Broad Street and follow that until you reach Ryan Street. End at **Sha Sha's of Creole** (609 Ryan St.; 337-494-7227). This local hot spot with Cajun favorites such as gumbo, crawfish, boudin, po'boys, and more will not disappoint.

NIGHTLIFE   After dinner, head south on Ryan Street and merge onto I-210 west. Take exit 4 to Nelson Road and follow Nelson Road to L'Auberge on Avenue L'Auberge. Not tired just yet? Grab a nightcap at **Globar,** a cool, circular bar located directly in the middle of L'Auberge's casino. Open Sun through Thurs until 4 a.m. and Fri and Sat twenty-four hours. One note: If you're gambling, cocktail waitresses will bring you free drinks. The casino also hosts seasonal events, such as a summer concert series held on Thurs called Party by the Pool and touring acts at its event center. The Jack Daniels Bar and Grill also regularly hosts karaoke and live performances Thurs through Sat.

DAY 3/MORNING

BREAKFAST Grab a quick bite at **Lattes** or visit **L'Auberge's Le Café,** which serves breakfast options around the clock.

It's time to head home, but on your way, be sure to stop at **Gator Country Wildlife Park** (off I-10 near Beaumont; 409-794-9453; www.gatorcountrytx.net). Even though it's technically across the Texas border, this attraction offers you one last opportunity to get a true taste of southwest Louisiana. Here, more than 180 American alligators are available for educational shows, photo ops, and even lunch—fried alligator is included on the menu. Call ahead for hours and admission.

There's More . . . .

Beach. **LaFleur Beach.** Popular beach located on Prien Lake near the I-210 bridge; (800) 456-7952.

Fun. **Adventure Cove.** Barrier-free playground with water features for children of various ages and abilities. 3200 Power Centre Parkway.

Gaming. **Isle of Capri Casino & Hotel.** More than 1,900 slots and 75 table games as well as live music, entertainment, food, and lodging. Exit 27 off I-10 in Westlake; www.isleofcapricasinos.com.

Golf. **Gray Plantation Golf Course.** Public eighteen-hole course with fantastic amenities. 6150 Graywood Parkway in Lake Charles; (337) 562-1663; www.graywoodllc.com.

Library. **Southwest Louisiana Genealogical and Historical Library.** The place to go for researching family histories in the area. 411 Pujo St.; (337) 721-7110.

Museums. **Brimstone Museum Complex.** Learn about the history of Sulphur, LA. 900 S. Huntington St.; (337) 527-0357.

Imperial Calcasieu Museum. Artifacts, art, and objects from this area's past designed to help preserve the culture of the region. 204 W. Sallier St.; (337) 439-3797.

Park. **Prien Lake Park.** Lakeside park with picnic area, boat launch, water features, and playground. 3700 W. Prien Lake Rd.; (337) 721-3500.

Race Track. **Delta Downs Racetrack Casino & Hotel.** More than 1,600 slots, plus off-track betting, and a horse track. Entertainment, food, and lodging are also available. Exit 4 or 7 off I-10 in North Vinton; (800) 589-7441; www.deltadowns.com.

Shopping. **Prien Lake Mall.** Shopping mall with eighty stores. 496 W. Prien Lake Rd.; (337) 447-7411; www.simon.com.

Spa. **Glam-N-Gloss Day Spa.** Full-service spa with facials, massages, pedicures, manicures, and more. 414 E. College St.; (337) 313-0222; www.glamandgloss.com.

Special Events & Festivals . . . .

JANUARY

Louisiana Fur and Wildlife Festival; Cameron. This annual event includes pageants, a gumbo cook-off, food, games, and more; http://lafurandwildlifefestival.com.

MARCH

Black Heritage Festival and Gallery, Lake Charles. An annual festival that features food, music, and arts and crafts vendors held at the Civic Center. (337) 488-0567; www.bhflc.org.

Southwest Louisiana Garden Festival, Lake Charles. A celebration of plants, gardening, and spending time outdoors; www.gardenfest.org.

APRIL

Louisiana Railroad Days Festival, DeQuincy. This festival includes a carnival, food booths, crafts, free entertainment, and a pageant; www.larailroaddaysfestival.com.

MAY

Contraband Days Pirate Festival, Lake Charles. The biggest festival in the region, this celebration of all things pirate is so popular it spans two weekends. Event includes music, pony rides, a bike ride, a car show, and a buccaneer raid on the shore; www.contrabanddays.com.

JULY

Marshland Festival, Lake Charles. Held at the Civic Center, this event features live Cajun, Zydeco, Swamp Pop, and country entertainers; www.marshlandfestival.com.

Other Recommended Restaurants & Lodgings . . . . .

LAKE CHARLES

Aunt Ruby's Bed and Breakfast, 504 Pujo St.; (337) 430-0603. Quaint, welcoming B&B located in the center of town.

Big Daddy's Sports Grill and Restaurant, 1737 W. Sale Rd.; (337) 477-9033. Burgers, seafood, steaks, and salads; also open for breakfast.

Dan's BBQ Express, 2635 Country Club Rd.; (337) 478-5858. Quick, tender barbecue.

Holiday Inn Express, 402 MLK Hwy.; (337) 491-6600. Affordable, centrally located lodging option.

The Landing, 1103 W. Prien Lake Rd.; (337) 478-7795. Casual, waterfront seafood restaurant with specials offered daily.

Mary Ann's Café, 110 Broad St.; (337) 436-9115. Solid, home-cooked breakfasts and lunches.

Snake River Grill, At L'Auberge du Lac, 777 Avenue L'Auberge; (337) 395-7777; www.ldlcasino.com. Fantastic steaks, wine, seafood, and more in a romantic, dimly lit restaurant.

Steamboat Bill's on the Lake, 1004 Lakeshore Dr.; (337) 494-1070; www.steamboatbills.com. Fantastic seafood in a gorgeous setting.

SULPHUR

The Sausage Link, 2400 E. Napoleon St. in Sulphur; (337) 625-8474. All things sausage, as well as boudin, seafood, burgers, and more.

For More Information . . . .

Lake Charles Convention and Visitors Bureau; www.visitlakecharles.org.

City of Lake Charles; www.cityoflakecharles.com.

CENTRAL ESCAPES

CENTRAL ESCAPE *One*
Unknown Houston
STAYCATION SENSATION: A NEW SIDE OF YOUR CITY / 2 NIGHTS

Shopping
Great restaurants
Outdoor scene
Live music
Artistic community

OK, I know what you're thinking. "I live in Houston. Why would I want a vacation here?"

Hear me out. Even if you've settled into a comfortable routine in this quaint town of four million, chances are there are still a lot of sides that you've never seen.

Houston is home to a huge artistic community as well as an amazing culinary scene. From odd museums to fantastic dessert shops to vintage stores with incredible finds, it's easy to uncover something new in Houston.

Here are my very favorite lesser known attractions in this fine town of ours.

DAY 1/MORNING

BREAKFAST Start your morning at the **Buffalo Grille** (3116 Bissonnet; 713-661-3663; www.thebuffalogrille.com), a West University–area institution known among residents of the neighborhood for one of the best breakfasts around. Founded in 1984, the restaurant, which considers itself the "Cheers" of Houston breakfast joints, continues to serve an impressive variety, from huevos rellenos to raspberry pancakes to build-your-own omelets. The best part? The prices are affordable and the food is really, really good.

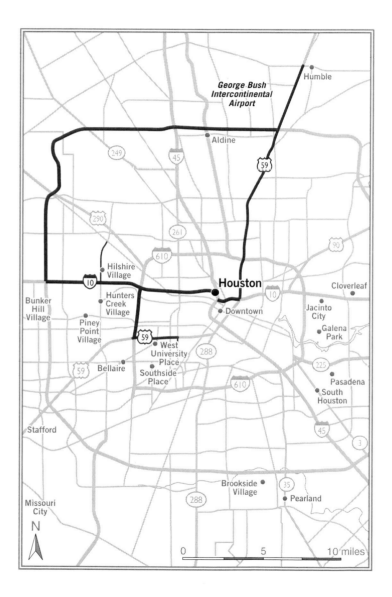

George Bush
Intercontinental
Airport

Humble

Aldine

249

45

59

290

261

90

610

Hilshire
Village

10

Houston

Cloverleaf

Hunters
Creek
Village

Downtown

10

Jacinto
City

Bunker
Hill
Village

Piney
Point
Village

Galena
Park

59

59

West
University
Place

288

225

Bellaire

Southside
Place

Pasadena

Stafford

610

South
Houston

45

3

Missouri
City

Brookside
Village

35

N

288

Pearland

0   5   10 miles

Next, head to **Memorial Park** (at the intersection of I-10 and I-1610; 713-863-8403; www.memorialparkconservancy.org) for some mountain biking. Memorial Park may be known for its popular 3-mile jogging loop, but did you know that it's also home to 1,500 acres of multiuse trails, including more than a dozen miles that are dedicated to mountain biking? The trails, which can include rocky terrain, steep inclines, and impressive downhills, are designated from easy to difficult by color-coded signs. Even though you're right next to two of the city's largest highways, the forestlike atmosphere of the park will make you feel far, far away. Don't have a bike? No worries. Rent one at the nearby **West End Bicycles** (5427 Blossom St.; 713-861-2271; www.westendbikes.com).

Then, take the short drive down Memorial Drive to **Buffalo Bayou** (713-752-0314; www.buffalobayou.org), a local bayou that runs from Katy to the Ship Channel. The Buffalo Bayou Partnership, which works to protect and support the portion of the bayou from Shepherd Drive to the Turning Basin, in recent years has started coordinating events such as the annual Buffalo Bayou Regatta, special festivals, and boat tours. Some of the most fun new additions to the bayou are hosted canoe and kayak trips, which are outfitted by North Lake Conroe Paddling Company and take place once or twice a month on Sat between 9 a.m. and 1 p.m. Call ahead for details or to sign up.

Next, head across Allen Parkway to the **Museum of Printing History** (1324 W. Clay St.; 713-522-4652; www.printingmuseum.org), a cool little museum where you can see a replica of the 1450 Gutenberg press, use an ink roller to create your own pages, and see newspapers detailing some of the country's most historic events. Open from 10 a.m. to 5 p.m. Tues through Sat. Admission is free.

LUNCH Head to the Midtown district for lunch at **Lankford Market** (88 Dennis St.; 713-522-9555), a quaint little restaurant with a small outdoor patio that serves one of the best burgers in Houston. It's gotten a little more crowded since it was featured on the Food Network's *Diners, Drive-Ins, and Dives*, but it's worth the wait. These juicy beauties and perfectly crisp fries have never let me down.

AFTERNOON

After lunch, head down the street to the **Texas Junk Co.** (215 Welch St.; 713-524-6257), where one person's junk really is another person's treasure. Featuring items such as glass bottles, vinyl albums, vintage mugs, and around 1,500 pairs of cowboy boots, this local institution will overwhelm you with its offerings. Don't be intimidated, though. Just take your time and dig around and you're bound to find something you like. Open from 11 a.m. to 6 p.m. Thurs through Sat.

Once you wrap things up there, cross the highway for a visit to the **John C. Freeman Weather Museum** (5104 Caroline; 713-529-3076; www.weathermuseum.org). Conveniently located near the Houston Children's Museum, the weather museum offers a range of activities for all ages. You can view terrariums representing various climates of the world, watch radar images of hurricanes that have impacted the coast, and even host your own weather forecast. Fans of Channel 2's former weather dog, Radar, will be happy to know that he also makes regular visits to the museum. Call ahead to see when he might be around. Open 10 a.m. to 4 p.m. Mon through Sat. Closed Sun. Admission is $5 for adults, $3 for students and seniors, and free for children 3 and under.

Now, it's time to head to the famous **Saint Arnold Brewing Company** (2000 Lyons Ave.; 713-686-9494; www.saintarnold .com) for a tour of the facility. Home to some of Texas's favorite beers, the brewing company switched venues in 2010 to a space near downtown that could accommodate a bigger operation (and more people during tours). Tours are offered on Sat from 11 a.m. to 2 p.m. and weekdays at 3 p.m. Cost is $7 and includes four samples, a souvenir tasting glass, and a tour of the facility. Coming with kids? Don't worry. There's plenty of Saint Arnold Root Beer on tap for them.

Next, cross over I-10 to **Minute Maid Park** (501 Crawford; 713-259-8000; www.mlb.com/hou/ballpark/directions.jsp), where even if it's not baseball season you can still tour the grounds where the Houston Astros spend their summers. A variety of tours are available, including a general tour, an early-bird tour (includes batting practice), and a clubhouse tour. Basic tours are offered Mon through Sat at 10 a.m., noon, and 2 p.m. and include visits to historic Union Station, a broadcasting booth or press box, the Astros' or visitors' dugout, luxury suites, and more. Cost is $9 for adults, $7 for seniors 65 and up, $5 for children 3–14, and free for children under 3.

DINNER For dinner, head over to a favorite Heights area eatery called **Cedar Creek** (1034 W. 20th St.; 713-808-9623; http://cedarcreek.squarespace .com), which manages to blend a Hill Country vibe with Houston's famous culinary tradition. Grab a seat at a picnic table outside next to the fountain and sip a local beer or cocktail from the full bar. Everything here, from the loaded salads to the fresh-off-the-grill sandwiches, is great. Don't miss the portobello burger, nachos, or kids macaroni and cheese. They're all fantastic.

NIGHTLIFE For a nightcap, go to one of Houston's seediest yet friendliest spots: **Marfreless** (2006 Peden; 713-528-0083; www.marfrelessbar.com). Known as Houston's "makeout bar," this dimly lit joint in River Oaks is recognizable only by its unmarked blue door. Downstairs, the bartenders are friendly, the martinis are strong, and the tables are less secretive—great if you want to meet friends or share a date night with a spouse. Upstairs, couches line a wide space where couples tend to get a little too close. Brave it if you dare.

LODGING For a great, centrally located lodging option, consider the **Alden Houston** (1117 Prairie St.; 832-200-8800; www.aldenhotels.com), a boutique hotel located downtown that features ninety-seven deluxe rooms and suites filled with amenities such as Wi-Fi, private voice mail, gourmet treats, 400-thread-count Egyptian cotton sheets, and Aveda bath and body products. On-site, enjoy an award-winning restaurant and bar as well as full meeting facilities.

DAY 2/MORNING

BREAKFAST Start your day by heading down Westheimer to **Brasil** (2604 Dunlavy St.; 713-528-1993), a funky cafe/coffee shop with a wonderful breakfast and lunch selection. The atmosphere here is laid-back and hip, and the food is fantastic, with menu items such as fresh-made quiche, pizza, sandwiches, and salad.

Next, go shopping at the boutiques on Westheimer, which range from vintage shops like **Taxi Taxi** (1657 Westheimer; 713-529-3742) to antiques shops like **B. J. Oldies** (1435 Westheimer; 832-651-8477; www.bjoldiesantiqueshop.com) to boutiques such as **Wish** (1614 Westheimer; 713-527-0812) to funky stores such as **FlashBack Funtiques** (1627 Westheimer; 713-522-7900; www.flashbackfuntiques.net). Should you get a little tired while you shop, drop by **Agora** (1712 Westheimer; 713-526-7212; www.agorahouston.com) or **Empire Café** (1732 Westheimer; 713-528-5282; www.empirecafe.com) for a quick latte or mocha.

Then, go a few streets over and visit **The Chocolate Bar** (1835 W. Alabama St.; 713-520-8599; www.theoriginalchocolatebar.com), a Willy Wonka-esque dessert shop dedicated to all things chocolate. Pick up a chocolate-covered Oreo, orange, or popcorn to go, or enjoy a scoop of homemade ice cream (favorite flavors include German chocolate, Nutter Butter, root beer float, and Candylicious Junkyard, a fantastic combination of favorite candy bars).

And don't miss the incredible cake selection in the adjacent dining room, where you can get gigantic slices of Turtle Torte, Bayou City mud pie, and Aunt Etta's fudge cake. Oh, and they also serve frozen hot chocolate, a New York fave turned Texan.

Also, be sure to also head next door to **Candylicious** (1837 W. Alabama St.; 713-529-6500), where you can find all of your favorite retro candy such as Pez, Bubble Tape, and every flavor of Jelly Belly you can imagine.

LUNCH For lunch, head to Midtown for some **Tacos A Go-Go** (3704 Main St.; 713-807-8226; www.tacosagogo.com), one of Houston's hippest, and best, taco joints. Don't let the kitschy decor, with its bright Tabasco mural and fun portraits of wrestling masks fool you—the cooks here know what they're doing. Menu items include carne guisada, barbacoa, chicken fajitas, and grilled fish tacos, as well as gorditas, tamales, fajitas, and breakfast tacos. Call for hours.

AFTERNOON

Taco-ed out? Go next door to the fantastic **Sig's Lagoon** (3710 Main St.; 713-533-9525; www.sigslagoon.com), which is always ready to impress with a huge vinyl record selection, tiki mugs, bobbleheads, collectibles, magnets, and more. If you have time, make sure to also check out the **Continental Club** (3700 Main St.; 713-529-9899; www.continentalclub.com), where great live music and cocktails are the order of the day.

Now, trek up US 59 north for one of the most unique experiences in Texas: **The DeLorean Motor Company** (15023 Eddie Dr. in Humble; 281-441-2537; www.delorean.com). If you've ever wished you could play *Back to the Future* and check out a DeLorean up close, here's your chance. The Motor Company services and remanufactures the famous car, which is no longer made, and offers tours of the facility as long as you book in advance. Decide you want to buy one? They can help you with that as well. For a cool $40,000, that is.

Then, take Beltway 8 west to I-10 until you reach the **Dairy Ashford Roller Rink** (1820 S. Dairy Ashford St.; 281-493-5651; www.skatedarr.com), another throwback venue that will take you right back to your formative roller-skating days. Come with the kids and enjoy rolling across the shiny wood floor, or visit during the evening for a date night: The rink is open to everyone. Concessions are available. Call ahead for hours and cost.

DINNER   For dinner, get your pizza fix in the Heights at **Star Pizza** (2111 Norfolk; 713-523-0800; http://starpizza.net). Located just off the hip Washington Avenue, Star is known for fantastic, thin-crust pies, with unique toppings including potatoes, cauliflower, Gorgonzola, sun-dried tomatoes, meatballs, and pesto, as well as all the usual suspects. Don't miss the delicious salsa verde focaccia pizza (tomatillo sauce with roasted poblano peppers, pan-fried garlic, and feta cheese) or the hand-tossed Starburst (ground beef, Italian sausage, pepperoni, onions, mushrooms, and green pepper). Open daily. Call for hours.

NIGHTLIFE   After dinner, dust off those cowboy boots for a night at **Blanco's** (3406 W. Alabama St.; 713-439-0072; www.houstonredneck.com), a little-known but much-loved dance hall/country bar with happy hour Mon through Fri, ladies night on Wed, and great local bands on Thurs. Closed most Sat and Sun, but call ahead to be sure.

DAY 3/MORNING

BREAKFAST   Start your day off right with a trip to the **Hot Bagel Shop** (2009 S. Shepherd Dr.; 713-520-0340; www.hotbagelshop.bravehost.com), a hole-in-the-wall bagel mecca that offers flavors including banana walnut, sea salt, onion garlic, oat bran raisin, strawberry, honey wheat, jalapeño, and more. Don't miss the flavored cream cheese, either. Call for hours.

There's More . . . .

Art. **Art Car Museum.** This tribute to Houston's favorite festival, the Art Car Parade, features a variety of uniquely decorated vehicles. 140 Heights Blvd.; (713) 861-5526; www.artcarmuseum.com.

Beer Can House. An oddly yet fabulously decorated house open for tours. 222 Malone St.; (713) 880-2008; www.beercan house.org.

The Orange Show. Another funky, fun, oddly decorated art house open for tours. 2402 Munger St.; (713) 926-6368; www .orangeshow.org.

Drive-In. **The Showboat Drive In.** Classic drive-in setup playing current movies. 22422 FM 2920 in Hockley; (281) 351-5224; www .theshowboatdrivein.com.

Nature. **Cactus King.** Huge garden/market with every type of cactus you can imagine. 625 W. Canino Rd.; (281) 591-8833; www.the cactusking.com.

Sports. **Houston Roller Derby.** Fast-paced action on a flat track. Bouts are held at the Verizon Wireless Theater downtown; www .houstonrollerderby.com.

Special Events & Festivals . . . .

FEBRUARY

Houston Livestock Show and Rodeo. One of the largest rodeos in the world, which lasts for nearly a month. Held in and around Reliant Center; www.hlsr.com.

MARCH
Bayou City Art Festival. Annual festival for art lovers in southeast Texas. Held in Memorial Park; (713) 521-0133; www.bayoucityart festival.com.

APRIL
iFEST. Celebrates a different area and culture each year with music, seminars, art, demonstrations, and more. Held in downtown Houston; www.ifest.org

MAY
Houston Art Car Parade. Annual parade of Houston's wackiest, tackiest, and most outrageous cars. Held downtown; www.orange show.org/artcar.html.

NOVEMBER
Nutcracker Market. Hosted by the Houston Ballet, the market includes more than 300 vendors. Held at Reliant Center; www .houstonballet.org.

Other Recommended Restaurants & Lodgings . . . . .

Hotel Derek, 2525 West Loop South; (866) 292-4100; www.hotel derek.com. Galleria-area hotel with great views.

Hotel Lancaster, 701 Texas; (713) 228-9500; www.thelancaster .com. Boutique hotel close to the Houston arts scene.

Hotel Zaza, 5701 Main St.; (713) 526-1991; www.hotelzazahouston .com. Sleek hotel in the heart of the Museum District.

Inversion Coffee, 1953 Montrose Blvd.; (713) 523-4866; www
.inversioncoffee.com. Coffee house in the heart of Montrose.

Kenny and Ziggy's, 2327 Post Oak Blvd.; (713) 871-8883;
www.kennyandziggys.com. New York–style deli with wonderful
sandwiches.

Magnolia Hotel, 1100 Texas Ave.; (713) 221-0011; www.magnolia
hotelhouston.com. Boutique hotel near Minute Maid Park.

Ninfa's on Navigation, 2704 Navigation Blvd.; (713) 228-1175;
www.ninfas.com. The original Ninfa's serves fantastic margaritas
and Tex-Mex.

Onion Creek Cafe, 3106 White Oak Dr.; (713) 880-0706; www
.onioncreekcafe.com. Fun, popular beer and wine spot.

Pesce, 3029 Kirby Dr.; (713) 522-4858; www.pescehouston.com.
Upscale, fresh seafood and delicious cocktails.

Pink's Pizza, 1403 Heights Blvd.; (713) 864-7465; www.pinks
pizza.com. Heights area pizza joint.

Spanish Flowers, 4701 N. Main St.; (713) 869-1706; www
.spanish-flowers.com. Tex-Mex joint open twenty-four hours.

Under the Volcano, 2349 Bissonnet St.; (713) 526-5282; www
.underthevolcanohouston.com. Fun bar with great food.

For More Information . . . .

Greater Houston Convention and Visitors Bureau, 901 Bagby, Suite 100; (713) 437-5200; www.visithoustontexas.com.

Hot Town Cool City. A log of quirky, interesting, and unknown Houston attractions; www.hottowncoolcity.org.

Houston Chronicle. City newspaper with local happenings; www.chron.com.

INDEX